Your Dad Didn't Have to Die

By Ford O'Kenaly

With & for Michael M. Hennelly

ISBN 978-1-62154-054-0

The following was constructed from what we could remember of the past. While each and every description may not be true in every detail, the events described contain a larger truth that we call emotional truth. These are the ways the memories presented themselves to us and grew in our minds as we dwelled on the past. We look forward to hearing from others who may remember things differently. We can learn from each other, just as we have learned from the reflection that went with the writing.

PROLOGUE -- WHO AM I

I am an old friend of your Grandfather. I have known him since he was quite young.

Our paths have crossed and crisscrossed again over the years. We have always been close. And we have always stayed in touch with one another.

Over the years, whenever we have come together, we would always "catch up" with each other. We have always known each other pretty well.

Your Granddad thought of me when he wanted to write to you.

From the time he heard of you he sensed there were things you should know. The problem was you were way too young to understand what he wanted to share. Another challenge for him was that there was so much to share.

How was he going to gets "things" out? With time much would be lost. Each day that passed made it harder for him to remember. He decided it was best to get what he wanted to share down on paper.

He asked if I would help him, and I agreed.

We – your Grandpa, in remembering, and I, in writing – have done our best to share with you. We hope you will become a better person as a result of what he has left for you. I would like to think that will be the case.

Read.
        Ponder.
                Consider.
                        Reflect.
                                And, finally, learn.

Your Dad Didn't Have to Die

By Ford O'Kenaly

With & for Michael M. Hennelly

TABLE OF CONTENTS

SECTION I -- YOUR DAD DIDN'T HAVE TO DIE

Chapter 1 -- JANUARY 17, 2012

It was a clear day and a crisp morning, as they often are in Prescott. The teacher was sick. So the class was held indoors.

Normally, the classes, particularly one such as this "Search and Rescue" class, were held outside.

It ended about midday. And a number of students in the class had the idea to go climbing.

Your Grandfather was told eight students from the class went together – rock climbing. They went to a place north of town. Actually, "town" had grown around the area, known as Granite Dells.

They had been climbing about three hours. It was mid-to-late afternoon, and they were in two groups.

Sean's group had started a climb from down in a ravine. Sean was in the lead. Matt H, not tethered to Sean, was below him. Cody was even further down at the bottom, holding the rope. I think it's called belaying.

Matt R was off to the side, around a corner, about 25 yards away, as were Matt W, Jordan, and Greg.

Ali was between Matt R. and Sean's group, on her way to climb with them.

The rope had gone around the highest previously-set anchor point. And Sean, your Dad, had climbed above that. Your Grandfather didn't know for sure, it seems maybe Sean was as high as 16 to 20 feet above that highest preset anchor.

The rock face wasn't smooth, but had ledges, or outcroppings. And at least two of those ledges were above that previously set anchor point.

It seems Sean was standing on one of those ledges, the upper one. That ledge, as best your Granddad can remember, was at least 8 to 10 feet above the other.

Sean was putting a "piece" into the rock; they call it a "cam". Or, he had just put the "piece" into the rock. Apparently, he was trying to extend the climb up, with another (higher) "anchoring" point.

Something happened. He slipped. He lost his footing. The cam didn't hold. He slid down.

His feet hit a ledge. He was flipping over backwards.

Still headed down.

Soon to be head first.

And backwards.

Like the crack of a whip, his head hit.

His head hit really hard.

It made a sickening sound. The sound a head makes when it hits something very, very hard. It was a dull, hard thud.

Your Granddad had heard that sound once, maybe twice, in his lifetime.

The head holds the brain, floating in water, surrounded by the skull.

Landing hard on the rock, when the skull cracks open, it can sound like a cantaloupe or a watermelon breaking open.

Your Granddad was told it all happened very fast.

Sean may have let out a sound.　But he was knocked unconscious.

He never woke up.

He died up there on the rocks.

Chapter 2 -- GOING TO SEAN: NOT YET AWARE OF
ALL THE MISTAKES

The next day, January 18th, he arrived. Sean's Dad, your Grandfather.

They had driven all night. Your Granddad Michael drove with three others: with Cindy, his new wife of only five months; with Sean's twenty-two year old sister, Maria-Teresa; and with Sean's mother, Louella.

It was about 8 am when they pulled into Prescott Valley.

They had left Albuquerque only six and a half hours earlier.

He had wanted to take his long-bed GMC truck. And he would have done so except that they found the backseat window on the driver's side shattered when they went to pack. Days later it was learned two vandals had driven through the neighborhood shooting out windows with a pellet gun.

Fortunately, Rebecca, sister to Sean's Aunt Veronica, who lived across the street, let them use her pickup truck. It was an extremely kind offering on her part. Your Grandfather saw it as a God-send.

Maria-Teresa had learned of her brother's death only six hours before they left Albuquerque. She was down in Las

Cruces, New Mexico, attending New Mexico State University.

Her cousin, Aunt Veronica's son, Paul, who was also in school there, was kind enough to drop everything and drive her up to Albuquerque from Las Cruces. It turns out, Mariah, that although they are cousins, Maria-Teresa and Paul are not really blood-related. Paul is Aunt Veronica's son by her first husband, who had died; not by her second husband, Sean's uncle and Louella's older brother.

After Maria-Teresa's arrival in Albuquerque, there was almost two hours more of preparation before they pulled out, sometime after 1:30 in the morning. And, as I mentioned, they drove all night.

Louella, almost immediately after learning of Sean's death, had been determined to get to Prescott as fast as she could. She kept asking your Grandfather to get an airplane ticket. She wanted to get on a plane and BE THERE immediately.

That made no sense to your Grandfather. Rushing to Prescott was not going to bring Sean back to life…

        back to life???

The words stuck inside your Grandfather. They weren't just words.

Part of him couldn't believe it.

He was stunned and numb.

Back to life??

Later, as she waited for Maria-Teresa to complete the three and a half hour drive up from Las Cruces, it dawned on Louella that Sean's "things" would need to be brought back from Prescott. Once she realized this, she was OK with driving over there, and no longer insisted on flying. Curiously, Sean's Dad told me that he just wouldn't have thought about Sean's things. Probably not until much later.

Your Granddad did most of the driving. And Louella did some.

They pulled into Prescott Valley, a little before 8 am, stopping there at a McDonalds for coffee and a bit of food. They all wanted something slightly different at that hour of the morning.

From there, he called Dean Jack Herring, of Prescott College. The Dean had talked with your Grandfather the evening before. The plan was to try to make it to Sean's class. Sean's "Search and Rescue" class.

The class was to start about 9 am. And some, if not most, of those who had been with your Dad the day before, would be there. Sean's Dad had realized, the evening before, when talking with the Dean, that those "kids" would be having a really hard time. How many of them had ever seen someone die? Much less their friend and classmate.

Not only did my friend want to know, from them, the details of the fall, but he also wanted to give them a chance to share. A chance to share with what was left of Sean.

14

What was left of Sean? What was still alive of Sean? His family. Who else could feel as they did -- about losing Sean?

He knew that those "kids", almost certainly, would benefit a great deal by talking and sharing. Sharing with "What was left of Sean."

You see, your Grandfather had lots of experiences around death. In his work as a doctor he had an unenviable familiarity with telling family and loved ones of death. Even before that, while in high school, he had worked at a Catholic cemetery. One of the death-related responsibilities there was to dig the graves and himself bury the little bodies of stillborns. In grade school he had frequently been called upon to act as alter-server at funerals. Each time this included the funeral Mass and a trip with the priest to the gravesite.

Those experiences of witnessing the tragedy of death in the lives of others taught him the solace so many grieving people sought if they could: to be near something or someone with some GREATER MEANING. He knew the importance of the Spirit within each person.

That drove him, as much or more than anything else, to get to Prescott in time to share with Sean's fellow students, many of them Sean's friends. He needed to share with their Spirits as much as they might need to share His.

Dean Herring, in that morning phone call, invited the four of them to meet at his office on the small campus before the class. They could all walk over to the classroom together.

It was about a 20 minute drive from Prescott Valley to the Prescott College campus. The four of them arrived there a few minutes early. They received his condolences and then the Dean suggested they might want to see a small shrine dedicated to Sean that had sprung up over night. The shrine was just across the used-to-be street from Dean Herring's office. It was in front of the Crossroads Center. Between the library and the café.

It was there that my good friend was first struck -- struck hard by the first of three additional blows that day. Since the night before he had been trying to grasp the reality that Sean, put simply, no longer existed – not within his body. Sean's death was unthinkable for him. Mariah, "unthinkable" is the best word I can come up with to describe to you what your Grandfather -- and my friend -- was experiencing.   Your Granddad is a man whose life revolves around thinking. Sean's death was beyond his ability to "think it through." Despite all of his experiences with death he was not prepared for his son's death. Sean's death was completely different for him than any death he had experienced or been close to. And, Mariah, the three blows he would experience the day after Sean's death would make the loss of Sean all the more unbearable for him.

Sean's death, and those three shocks, would weigh on his mind -- and on his soul -- for the remainder of his life.

This first blow came at the little shrine.

You might be able to physically see what he saw that morning, at the little shrine. There are some pictures of the little memorial. I will try to add one of the pictures to this book for you to see. But you are not likely to see with the same understanding he did. I don't think you can realize what he realized until you know this story that I am telling.

The story is Sean's story. And it's your Granddad's story; my friend's story.

When you know the story, then you will better understand your Dad and your Granddad. And you will better understand that first day after Sean's death. And you will better understand what keeps going on – what keeps churning - inside of that Grandfather of yours.

Maybe, also, you will better understand your life. And maybe, also, you will be better prepared to live your life. Your life without your Dad.

Chapter 3 -- A CHANCE FOR SEAN ??

It was late December of 2008, when your Grandfather went up from Albuquerque to Santa Fe to visit his sister, Kathleen. He had been busy with his own responsibilities and, thus, he had not seen her over the Christmas holidays. He wanted to share with her before the end of the year.

Early in their visit, he asked her about her children. As she shared, he learned about his nephew (her son, Kyle), and what he was going through. My friend told me that he felt badly. As had been too often the case in his life, he was very busy. Indeed, he had been so busy with his own "things" that he had not realized what his nephew and his sister were going through.

It turned out that Kathleen's son was, or had been, in a wilderness program.

What was that? What's a wilderness program? And why had he needed to go?

It seems that after Kyle's father, "Uncle Duff", had died, Kyle went into a depression. And, in addition, he had started using alcohol. Kathleen told her brother, your Granddad, how she couldn't find a way to reach him. And how he had become disobedient, headstrong, and unmanageable. It seemed he had developed alcoholism.

Whew! Your Grandfather felt horrible. For Kyle, for his sister, for what they were going through. And for not staying in touch with them.

He listened intently. In the process, he learned this wilderness program had moved his nephew in such a way that he became more aware of himself and his problems. She told her brother how Kyle was now able to go on, in a positive way, with his life. And how he was growing.

My friend was both intrigued and envious. He had been wondering for many years if there was anything he could do to help his own son, Sean. Your Grandfather had always had his antennae out, looking for some way to help.

As they visited more, he wondered, out loud, to his sister: "I sure wish there was some kind of program like that for Sean to get into. But he is 23 years old. How can there be a program for 'kids' over 18, particularly when a parent can't legally force them to go?"

Kathleen responded she thought there were such programs, for young adults over 18.

Even if there was, getting Sean to accept such help -- and to voluntarily go and to participate -- was another issue.

Sean's Dad wanted to believe there was such a possibility. A glimmer of hope came up inside of him. I knew, as his friend since childhood, how he had suffered in despair for years worrying about Sean. Sean had rejected, and continued to reject, virtually any suggestion or recommendation from his Dad.

Your Granddad sat there in Santa Fe with his sister and pondered the possibility. He allowed himself to consider it. He shared his thinking with her. She listened. She encouraged him as he scanned his mind, wondering how to make such a possibility into a reality.

This is something that came naturally to your Granddad --
scanning his mind for opportunities to help others. As a
physician, he had worked for years with mostly
underprivileged patients. When he and his sister were
younger, those kinds of patients were just called "poor"
patients. Many of those patients could not see or find
possibilities in their own lives. Your Grandfather would
help them find possibilities. Possibilities for better health.
Possibilities for a better life. He was, by nature, a problem
solver and a helper.

As he pondered things, it dawned on him. Sean was, at that
very moment, locked up in a detention center in
Albuquerque. He had been locked up for another DWI –
Driving While Intoxicated. That might be the key.
Ironically, Sean's being locked up might be just what his
Dad needed to help him.

Sean's arrests had started in high school. They always
involved alcohol or drugs. In the beginning, your
Granddad had helped Sean with the arrests. But he wasn't
involved in this one. Over the years Sean had kept lying.
He would promise to change, but he wouldn't. Sean wasn't
honest with himself or with others.

Sean had never paid his Dad back for the help. Over and
over your Granddad had helped. Sean would never keep
his promises. It was never clear to me why my friend
continued to help while Sean seemed to be manipulating
him. It didn't seem Sean would ever put any real effort
into trying to change.

Sean had a very bad attitude. Sean was cocky. He thought
he was tough. Sean prided himself into thinking he could
manipulate the police and the legal system: self-deception.

Sean would even brag he could handle himself in prison if he had to.

So, when your Grandfather had heard of the latest DWI arrest he thought: "Why should I even try to help my son?"

You see, it was Sean's mother who had been supporting him. After Sean flunked out of college she took him in. He had lasted only one semester. He had partied instead of studying.

She would enable Sean. She provided him a place to stay. She made sure he was clothed. That he had access to transportation. She even made sure his cell phone was paid for. And if he found odd jobs and ways to make a few dollars she let him keep enough money to pay for his cigarettes, booze, and drugs. Why should he change?

Sean's mother wouldn't listen to his Father. Neither she nor Sean would listen to your Granddad. They didn't seem to respect him.

She would indirectly but repeatedly insult your Grandfather. He would try to talk with her about the serious problems Sean was facing. She would repeatedly claim he was exaggerating things and the issues were "no-big-deal."

And Sean had developed the same attitude.

That's the kind of life Sean had lived for about four years, ever since he flunked out of college. That's the kind of life that led to his most recent DWI arrest and lock up.

Years earlier, when Sean was in high school, his mom had refused to help Granddad with Sean and his problems. She lived in Phoenix. My friend had the kids alone in Albuquerque. She refused to move back and help when asked.

It was during those high school years, when Sean's father began to learn the personal challenges of living with an alcoholic that he loved.

By the time of this latest DWI arrest, Sean's Dad had come to realize that if Sean wasn't forced to face the consequences of his choices and decisions, then he would never change for the better. His mother, unfortunately, had not learned that lesson and never would come to that realization; tragically so.

With all this going through his mind, my friend's logic went this way:

> "Sean is no longer under my legal authority. He is 23 years old. I can't force him to go anywhere. Kyle is under 18, he had to go when Kathleen had forced him to do so.

> "Sean would rebel at anything suggested by me, his father. With the image painted in his mind by his mother, I am the enemy. Anything I would suggest to help Sean must be rejected.

> "But, what if the judge...   what if the court... gave Sean a choice?

> "Maybe...   just maybe...   there was a chance to help him.

"A wilderness program. Hhhmmm…. Sean loved the outdoors. Time in the outdoors had to trump time in the detention center or jail!"

There was a glimmer of hope.

Sean's Dad decided to contact the educational consultant, as his sister, Kathleen, had suggested. Yep, it was an "educational consultant." That was the term she had used for the person who had helped her to intervene for her son, Kyle.

A day later he called the consultant. The advisor listened intently to his outline of Sean's present situation and his past history. To his surprise, she thought there was a chance to help him.

My friend's heart lightened… at least a tiny bit. The burden of worry about his son, with no concrete way to help him, had weighed on his mind -- and on his soul -- all the time. Her optimism shifted that burden even if just a little. There might be a chance to help Sean. Maybe Sean could be helped onto a different path, and out of the self-destruction he was living. This was cause for hope, if not joy. But only if it could be realized.

My friend forced an appointment, to meet personally with the consultant, Kim Rubin, into his busy work schedule. A day or so later he drove back up to Santa Fe, and met with her.

He spent 2-3 hours explaining everything to her. He was amazed by her interest in all the details. She wanted to know all about Sean's life. All of his problems. All about his problems. Everything.

She listened and learned about Sean's struggles with dyslexia. How he had to sacrifice so much during his junior high school and early high school years, in order to learn how to read.

My friend's eyes watered with tears as he told her about that. It caused him great sadness just to remember what Sean must have experienced in those years. He knew that so much of the suffering could have been avoided, if only Sean had had the support of a united team of parents

She listened and learned about how the Attention Deficit Disorder was belatedly recognized. And then how Sean, often with his mother's support, resisted treatment for this. Many of the very treatments your Grandfather had repeatedly prescribed to help his own patients with ADD were opposed or rejected.

The consultant then listened and learned how the problems with alcohol and marijuana had surfaced and grown.

Surprisingly, to Sean's Dad anyway, she seemed to accept the story. It was as if she had heard it before. That was both painful and hopeful for him.

Painful: because Sean's story was apparently not as unique as the pain made his father feel.

Hopeful: because her familiarity gave him a sense that she understood.

And, although he hadn't consciously realized it until that moment, my friend had come to believe there wasn't anyone else on the face of the earth who could really understand what he knew about his son. No one else could comprehend all of Sean's needs and all he had suffered. How could they? If someone as close as Sean's mother could not grasp what Sean was facing, feeling, and wrestling with, how could anyone who was unrelated understand? That was what your Grandfather had come to subconsciously believe.

He was deeply moved, especially when she told him she thought there was a way to help Sean.

He was both excited to believe her and afraid to believe her.

He had prayed for a chance to help his son -- for years. He had seen Sean self-destructing and he couldn't stop it. Despite being rejected by Sean and by his mother, he had constantly hoped. Despite his estranged distance from Sean for over 4 years, he had repeatedly scanned his mind for some way to effectively help his son -- his son, whom he loved so very much.

Chapter 4 -- HELPING SEAN, A START

So here was a chance. Here was a possibility of helping Sean.

But it would need the support of the judge.

Without the support of the judge, your Granddad knew, there was NO WAY Sean would agree to any help.

The educational therapist suggested he hire a lawyer – to work with the judge. Lawyers can be expensive, he thought. Up to this point your Grandfather hadn't thought about what this help for Sean might cost. He knew he wanted Sean to grow and to change. He just had not had time to think about the financial side of this undertaking. Now she was talking about an expensive lawyer. And what about the price tag for her help?

Your Grandfather began to think in broad financial terms. He knew he was already WAY behind in saving for retirement. He knew that years of covering for his wife's overspending and years of under-earning by himself (due to the troubles and discord in the marriage) and years of educational therapy for Sean (for his dyslexia) and years of private education for the children – those things had combined to put him way behind financially.

At that moment he couldn't imagine paying for a lawyer. (Little did he know his decisions to help Sean over the next four years were going to drain him of many more tens of thousands of dollars. Money he had tried to save for retirement continually seemed to dwindle away....) He thought he could do it without hiring a lawyer.

She, the educational consultant, thought your Grandfather was nuts to try this intervention without alone. But he still had some of the spunk that he had lots of in his youth. Besides, he had three siblings who were lawyers, and they might be willing to help him out, if need be.

Then there was the question of timing. Sean was not going to be locked up in the detention center indefinitely. And, paradoxically, it was Sean being locked up that gave his Dad any leverage at all.

Your Granddad initially planned to call the judge. After reflecting, he decided it was better to see the Judge in person. It would be another two days until he could get off work, but he sensed the odds of success increased considerably if could talk with the Judge face-to-face. He made up his mind to sit and wait for an opening with the Judge all day if that's what it took to get a moment of the judge's time.

You know, Mariah, it has been several years and your Granddad couldn't remember the exact details. But somehow he managed to get that judge to meet with him. The judge even allowed him into his private office area in the courthouse. There Grandpa laid out the situation. It was a story he had rehearsed over and over in the days since the idea had been hatched in Santa Fe.

He was pleasantly surprised when the judge listened to the whole story with barely an interruption. My friend found a way to summarize or outline Sean's difficulties since the second grade. Learning difficulties. The discovery of dyslexia. The search for treatment. The sacrifices Sean had to make to learn to read. The problems of self-image. Teenage troubles. Flunking out of college. Wandering for years -- with drugs and alcohol. Now the 3rd DWI.

To his surprise the judge then shared his own story. The judge had lost his own son, tragically, as a result of drugs and alcohol. The judge was very sympathetic. He agreed to work with Grandpa, to "conspire" with him, you might say. Together they would present Sean an option or an offer. One he would find difficult to refuse. Preparing all the legal papers would take a few days. They needed to move along efficiently.

Mariah, I think it is important for you to know Sean's Dad had invited Louella to participate in all of this. Indeed, the moment he left the first meeting with the educational consultant, Kim Rubin, he called Louella. He was excited for Sean and wanted so badly to share this opportunity and good fortune with her, his mother. He couldn't imagine her not wanting to work together for Sean's benefit.

That hope was soon deflated. Sadly, she was far from enthusiastic. She immediately made it clear she was not going to pay any money for anything. Not to anyone, and not for any help or treatment for Sean. And Grandpa hadn't said a word about money to her. She said maybe, if she had time, she might go talk to Ms. Rubin.

My friend was deeply hurt and disappointed by her negativity. Why he felt that way didn't entirely make sense, however. You see, from my point-of-view, Louella had never been very supportive. Over the years, she had refused one positive suggestion of Granddad's after another. She hadn't just been discouraging; she had been downright negative. That seemed especially true when it came to helping Sean. Yet he continued to be surprised when she would not "get on board" as he called it. It was as though my friend believed one day she would finally "get it." He kept expecting her to come to an understanding and that a "light bulb was going to go on in her head."

This was hard for me, as his friend. I sensed he was making a misjudgment about her. But I saw him do it over and over.

Well, in any case, he proceeded undeterred. I found him to be energized in a way I had not seen him in years. He would tell me, over and over, how grateful he was to God for answering his prayers and for giving him this chance to help his son. He was inspired.

He poured himself into the project. He spent scores of hours talking to different people and preparing papers. He laid out Sean's past for those who would be working with Sean and helping him. He did all of the legal or technical things the judge asked or needed.

I remember him saying, during this period of intense effort, that someone very close to him made the statement "I guess I have to get a DWI to get some of your time." That person was suggesting my friend might be rewarding Sean for his bad behavior. This hurt him deeply. He thought "Wouldn't anyone do everything they could to help their own child?" But, at the same time, it made him realize just how much time and energy he was spending in this struggle.

As I said, he saw this as an answer to his prayers. Finally, he had a chance to help his son, who was so tormented and confused.

Mariah, when I started this story, I didn't realize there was so much to share. But I have come to believe that for you to understand your Grandfather, and what he experienced that day after Sean's death -- and what he's had to live with all the days since then -- I need to get down on paper as much as I can remember.

Besides, and maybe more importantly, in this sharing you will learn about your Dad. You will learn much about his life. You will be able to understand much of the suffering he must have experienced. And, I hope, you will be able to see how so much of that suffering could have been avoided.

Also, your Granddad made me promise. He made me promise to explain everything that I could. He wanted to protect you, at least as much as he could. He felt that if you didn't know a lot of these things, then you would be at risk of experiencing some of the same things. And he wanted to keep you from any unnecessary suffering.

Your Grandfather thought of you as a part of Sean. He had begun to care about you just as he cared about his son.

So, let me go on with the story.

Well, the educational consultant was hired. And a series of communications followed. She thought it important to have Louella's support. When she learned from Sean's

Dad about Louella negative response to the opportunity, she offered to initiate talk with Louella to try to get her on board. But Louella put forth no effort to in response to Ms. Rubin's attempts. When that failed, Kathleen, who was on good terms with Louella, offered to try to explain to her the intervention and its importance for Sean. They spoke. Still, Louella declined to participate. She rejected Kathleen's experience and suggestions just as she had your Granddad's and Ms. Rubin's. Louella would have no part of this.

They proceeded without her.

When it became clear the judge was supportive, the educational consultant discussed with your Granddad the details of transporting Sean from the custody of the detention center to the custody of the treatment program.

She convinced him Sean should have SOMEONE OTHER THAN HIS DAD escort Sean to the wilderness program. He hated to part with more money, but it didn't take much for him to realize she was correct. For years, when Sean and his Dad spent time together, Sean's pattern of dysfunction and disrespect and anger and frustration and projection onto his Dad would repeat. Sean would get feelings he hadn't learned to process and control. There was no reason to believe it would be different now. And, if that pattern repeated itself, there was a good chance Sean would bolt. And that would cause Sean more problems, not less.

Remember, the court was allowing Sean out of jail not to be free or at liberty. Sean would be allowed to leave the detention center with the understanding he would go directly into a treatment program.

By the way, your Grandfather came to understand how lucky he was, and Sean was, to have this particular Judge. You see, at that time (and maybe since then) there were few people to come before any judge in New Mexico (a poor state) who had the resources to consider such a program. It seems that the judges – at least here in New Mexico -- were not familiar with such programs. From the point of view of a judge, releasing someone to the responsibility of others was risky. If the individual in detention, in this case Sean, was allowed out of custody, and then he ran away and did something stupid or dangerous or illegal, then the judge could be held responsible. That could make the judge look like a fool. And judges in NM are elected by the public, not appointed.

So, you can see how fortunate Sean, and his Dad, were, to happen upon this particular Judge with the guts to take a risk.
The program Sean would be headed for was in southern Utah. It was decided the best way to get him there was through the airport in Las Vegas, Nevada.

Chapter 5 -- GETTING TO STEP ONE

A woman named Twila, who worked with Ms. Rubin, the educational consultant, had been suggested to escort Sean to Las Vegas. She had experience with such interventions. She met with your Granddad. And, he was impressed by her kindness and clarity of thinking, particularly toward those with drug and alcohol problems. She seemed to sense how and when to be firm and how and when to be kind. That is what your Grandfather thought, anyway. He agreed with Ms. Rubin's suggestion, and he hired her.

Her plane ticket had to be purchased – round trip. Sean's too – one way.

The legal paper work had to be precise. If the attendants at the detention center were not certain about what they were to do, and they balked, then the planned sequence of events could fall apart. Your Grandfather had reviewed all the papers with the judge a few days earlier and had them ready for Twila on the day of planned transfer.

I don't know how my friend was able to get all those kinds of things done and still put in a full work week. But he did. He had always worked hard.

On the planned transfer day, Sean's Dad was worried. He knew this might be the only chance he would get to help Sean. And, he was afraid that once Sean understood the program's emphasis on treatment and not on "wilderness" he might back out. Sean had to agree to go. No one could force him.

Sean had always been afraid of treatment. It seemed to your Grandfather that his son's thinking went like this. If Sean ever agreed to treatment, then he was agreeing he had something wrong with himself. And Sean did not want to accept something was wrong with himself. (That prideful fear started years earlier. I hope to share with you about that later.)

Sean wanted any problems to be "out there" – that is, outside of himself. At this point in his life and in emotional development, Sean was not going to take on any responsibility or ownership for his problems. Since his Father was the one who would bring up problems and want Sean to deal with them, Sean felt his Father had the problem. Or, better yet, his Father *was* the problem. As Sean saw things, Grandfather should just leave the problems alone; they were "no-big-deal." (If you wonder how Sean came to that backward way of thinking, read on. You see, that confused way of dealing with life and its challenges is a big part of what your Granddad thinks is very important for you, Mariah, to understand and avoid.)

One of the other possible obstacles to a successful intervention and transfer was Sean's mom. Remember, she had refused your Grandfather. She had refused Ms. Rubin. And she had refused Aunt Kathleen. No one could get her to budge. She had refused to get involved. She had refused to help. And she could choose to undermine efforts and convince Sean to refuse to participate. They had to be realistic about her position, and the risk she posed.

Mariah, you have to ask yourself: Why? Why would a mother not want to help her son? This is one of those questions that still haunts your Granddad, as it would anyone else who was involved or understood the situation and circumstances.

When transfer day came, your Grandfather met Twila in the parking lot of the detention center. He went over each of the papers with her.

One of the papers had legal instructions to the detention center attendants giving them formal permission to release Sean to Twila. Actually these "attendants" were "guards", but I believe it was still hard for your Granddad to think of Sean as being in jail. He always had this sense that Sean needed treatment, not punishment.

Another of the papers documented Twila had the court's permission to escort him to the program. That was needed in case they got stopped for some reason, or in case Sean did something stupid, bad, or illegal.

I think your Granddad mentioned a third paper authorizing Sean to be in the program. All very legal. Sean was getting special permission only to be "on leave" from his detention. Technically, he was still in custody.

After all was discussed, Sean's Dad left the rest to Twila. She promised to call him and let him know how things were going, particularly if anything went wrong.

Your Granddad drove home and waited. She went into the detention center to get Sean.

Granddad and Twila had estimated 45 minutes to an hour for the release. They had set aside plenty of time after that, for Twila and Sean to get to the airport. They did not want anything to cause the flight to be missed.

They anticipated Sean would be "all questions". Remember, there had not been phone access to Sean, while he was in the detention center. All the details and preparations were made without his involvement. This was partly due to the lack of phone contact and partly intentional. The plan was to have as much as possible in order before Sean agreed to attend. Then, in a matter of only several days, the transfer would occur. That way he wouldn't have time to change his mind and back out. There was a realistic fear the patterns of the past would be repeated. That he would once again refuse care. And that all the effort and potential to help him would be lost.

One of the major "patterns of the past" also had to do with Sean's mother. Kim Rubin and Twila were convinced Louella might try to subvert the plan, based on her past choices as well as her present refusal to participate.

In the past Louella had repeatedly enabled Sean. "Enabled" is a term used in addiction care. As Sean's "enabler", she would repeatedly protect him from the consequences that normally should have resulted from his poor choices and bad behavior. And Sean was dependent on her for that protection.

Moreover and in addition, she seemed to have made it a point to oppose almost everything that your Grandfather had suggested or tried to do to help Sean.

I think your Granddad told me this pattern of maternal behavior is referred to New Mexico as the "Mi Hijito Syndrome" or the "Mi Pobre Hijito Syndrome". Your

36

Grandpa had learned of this pattern of behavior in Spanish-American mothers in New Mexico when he was in training at the University of New Mexico years earlier. Later, his brother Kevin, who worked as a psychologist for many years in Northern New Mexico, also became familiar with this pattern of maternal behavior. Mothers would "enable" their adult sons, protecting them from consequences and responsibilities of their choices. The son's maturation into an adult male was thereby arrested or halted.

But, you know, paradoxically, I don't believe my friend "saw" or recognized that pattern or syndrome in his own family at that time. I believe he was just too close to the situation, being father to one and husband (or ex-husband, at the time) to the other.

In any case, lots of things needed to go "just right" for this intervention to succeed.

Fortunately, Sean and Twila made it out of the "D-center" without a hitch.

As expected, we later learned, the questions from Sean started. Twila handled them smoothly. No arguments. No conflict. Calm reassurance.

Sean was, understandably, anxious.

What was he headed for? What had he actually agreed to?

They went to the airport.

The flight was delayed.

What does Sean want when he is anxious?

He had been given back his pocket cash when leaving the detention center. He went to buy a beer.

Twila did not protest. Her goal was to get him to treatment – sober, or not.

Then, in the delay at the airport, he called his mom. Your Grandfather assumed Sean quickly established in that conversation with her, that Louella was not a participant in this intervention. She was not a part of the plan to get him into the program.

As expected, the pattern of interaction between mother and son resumed. Louella commiserated with him and his plight. She felt sorry for him.

How did your Grandpa learn this?

Well, immediately after talking with Sean, Louella had called his Dad. And instead of praising Grandpa for all the time and effort it took to get to this point, she pleaded with him to STOP THE INTERVENTION.

In addition, Mariah, she tried to use YOU as a weapon to emotionally beat your Grandfather into changing his mind and into keeping your Dad out of treatment!

Let me explain.

Remember, Louella had had weeks to talk with people – Kim Rubin, the educational consultant; Aunt Kathleen, who had been through this with Kyle; Sean's Dad who had invited her into the solution; as well as the director of the wilderness program. She had repeatedly declined to get involved in any way.

What was she thinking? Or not thinking? Whatever it was, it made no sense to my friend.

Well, on the phone that day, with Sean and Twila waiting for the delayed flight, and in a huffy, demanding voice, Louella told Sean's Dad that he "couldn't do this." By "this" she meant carry out Sean's intervention.

"Why?" Granddad asked, as he tried once again to explain to her how this could help your Dad.

She would have none of it.

And, it was then that she told him of you. She declared that "Sean is about to be a father." She claimed that because of this Sean should remain here in New Mexico to be around for the forthcoming birth.

Your Grandfather was dazed. No one had told him of a pregnancy.

But, he immediately rebounded and realized that this had been the pattern for years. Louella had taught Sean to lie to your Granddad. Maybe this fatherhood claim was true and maybe it was not. In either case, at this point that did not matter. Your Grandfather quickly began to reason "If this is true, what is the best thing for that child?"

He told Louella something to this effect "Look, Sean can't even take care of himself. He hasn't had a steady job of any worth in years. He has no education. He has been freeloading off of you. He is not dealing with his alcoholism. And now he has trouble with the law. How is he going to be any good for a child? The best thing for any child of his would be for him to get the help he needs, so he can make something of his life."

My friend was even more determined that he was doing the right thing.

Meanwhile, back at the airport, Sean was going for his second beer. His preferred method of dealing with stress: alcohol (or drugs).

Twila was "cool," as they say. She remained calm, in the face of the delay, and Sean's drinking, and Sean's protests. Your Grandfather realized he could have never stayed calm if he saw Sean go straight to beer. He realized he had done the right thing in hiring Twila to escort Sean.

Finally, the time arrived for the flight, and there were no further calls from Twila. It was reasonable for your Granddad to assume they had boarded the plane and headed for Las Vegas.

So far, so good.

It would be hard for Sean to back out now.

Sean's Dad let out a big sigh of relief.

Now his brain could start to digest the claim: Sean was going to be a father.

Problem: (a) he couldn't trust Louella or Sean and (b) he couldn't talk, in any meaningful way, with either.

This was because....

Well, Mariah, you will just have to read on to better understand.

Hopefully you will see how each of them would have to change before your Grandfather would be able to have a meaningful and honest talk with either of them.

Chapter 6 -- ONE TOUGH KID

Sean was walled off - emotionally.

Sean was not about to admit he needed anybody's help.

Remember, in his mind, Sean didn't have any problems.

Other people might have problems, but not him.

If his Dad would just leave him alone he would get along fine.

If the cops and the judges would leave him alone, he was just fine, thank you very much.

As I told you before, Mariah, Sean believed he could get along in jail if he had to go there. On the outside, at least, he wasn't afraid. And, maybe, he was at least partially right. By that point in his life most of the people he hung out with were alcoholics and/or drug addicts. At least some of them had spent time in jail or in prison. They had taught him some things about living life behind bars.

In any case, he had convinced himself he could handle life no matter what others threw at him. He thought he was tough.

Psychologists might have said he was "defended". He had built an unconscious, interior wall to protect himself from the emotional pain.

Sean decided to go to that wilderness program because he would rather be outside in nature rather than inside a detention center. However, he had no interest in changing. He had no interest, at all, in "therapy."

Nobody was going to teach him anything.

He believed he knew all that he needed to know about life.

He also believed he knew all about living outside in the woods, even in the dead of the Utah winter. He knew as much, he thought, as the people who were running the wilderness program.

On that issue, he might not have been so far off either.

Your Grandfather came to learn later that the counselors and therapists at the program, called Second Nature, had been a bit anxious about Sean. They thought he might actually be someone who had the where-with-all to safely hike out of the wilderness on his own, despite the winter.

Rules: who needed rules? Sean surely didn't.
(Unfortunately, he didn't completely get over that attitude. And that attitude played a role in his fatal decisions on the day of his death.)

One of the rules of this wilderness program was to declare and to give up, when you started, any matches or lighters. As these could be used to start a fire, having them could make it easier for someone to run off and escape the wilderness and the program.

Your Dad was a smoker (unfortunately). And, thus, he had a lighter.

Well, he didn't "declare" his lighter.

And after a few days the lighter was "found out" by fellow enrollees and, subsequently, by the counselors.

What to do?

Part of the therapy of the program, a big part of the therapy, was peer driven. One of the techniques was to have individuals share life events. Sometimes these were around a bonfire. Virtually always they were in a circle.

In addition, there were also semi-spontaneous, yet still partially structured sharings, when someone felt the need to speak up and to be heard; or to get something out that was festering inside.

Within a few hours of arrival in the wilderness Sean would have experienced, already, several such sessions.

New arrivals were expected to share their stories with the group – sooner or later. Individuals in the group would then ask questions for clarification and/or share observations. Remember, each of the persons enrolled was there for a reason. Often, but not always, the reason revolved around alcohol or drugs. The counselors kept the sessions "on track." That is, they were trained to keep the sharing helpful, positive, and/or instructive; not condemning, negative, or destructive.

Sean was not the least bit interested in sharing. And he didn't. For days, your Grandfather was told, Sean declined to share "his story."

But he heard others. In the sessions, he heard, repeatedly, what had happened in the lives of others; the things that "got them here." And he heard how others were wrestling with "those things." One person after another, little by little, day after day would talk and share. Feelings and emotions came out. Hurting and having been hurt.

Sean was convinced he was different. He wasn't like the others. He didn't have those problems and he sure didn't have those feelings or emotions.

As I said, he was "defended." He was emotionally walled off.

He tolerated the listening, but that was only because he couldn't "get away" from the words.

Weekly his Dad would talk with the therapist.

The program was having a hard time with Sean. The therapist described how Sean wouldn't open up. He had lots of denial.

.

Fortunately, your Grandfather's background, as a family doctor, had given him opportunity to be able to understand what was going on.

Years before, your Granddad had decided to serve the people of a small town. This town and its surrounding area were made up of people who didn't have much economically. In addition, many of them didn't have the experience or capacity to easily understand or deal with psychological and emotional problems.

So, Sean's Dad, in order to help them, had to learn much more about mental and emotional illness than many of his physician colleagues.

That knowledge was very fortunate because Sean's resistance went on for weeks. Through the slow process, Sean's Dad stuck with the program and he stuck with Sean.

But don't think this was easy for him. This period was very, very difficult and painful.

It was also very expensive. He was paying almost $3,500 per week. And I already shared with you some of the financial stress he felt.

During all of this my friend had little emotional support for himself. His family and friends had their own children and issues to deal with. And, obviously, he couldn't lean on Sean's mother for support. She was making things more difficult, not easier.

On top of all this, my friend knew he himself was a part of Sean's problem. He knew he had to change if Sean was to have a chance at turning his life around. It wasn't yet clear to your Grandfather what he was doing wrong but his physician's knowledge and experience told him it was the people around Sean that had led Sean into the confusion and mistakes. Or, at least, the people around Sean played a role in keeping Sean from finding a healthy, constructive way to deal with the challenges life and God had given to him. Clearly, my friend had to accept that he himself was one of those people.

So, while Sean was resisting change, his Dad was doing all he could to understand his role in Sean's issues. He would read all he could from the program's resources for parents. They had an "on-line" library. He was determined to do what he could to change if that would help his son.

Chapter 7 -- THE BEGINNINGS OF CHANGE

The therapist who worked most with Sean was a guy named Mike Hench.

While Sean pushed the limits of the program, Mike Hench was patient and probing. And he eventually found a way to reach Sean – emotionally.

Remember the lighter Sean had kept? Remember how I told you the counselors were told Sean had the lighter?

Well, that became a recurrent issue. The other students / enrollees / patients / clients (or, as Sean might have considered them: inmates) would repeatedly challenge the counselors and the therapist to take the lighter from Sean. They wanted those in authority to enforce the rules.

Mike Hench was much more insightful. He turned the issue back on Sean.

What did Sean think he should do? Sean could share his thoughts with others in the circle sharing. And the others would share their thoughts and feelings with Sean.

Why did they think and feel as they did?

As you can imagine, Sean initially was content with breaking the rules and keeping his lighter. Indeed, Sean seemed to savor his role as a successful dissenter.

Mike Hench was a smart man, according to your Grandfather. He was able to see Sean's strengths right through his defenses. And, Mike Hench focused on the goal: how to get Sean to open up emotionally.

Mike, and the counselors working under him, began to praise Sean for his good qualities. This was honest and legitimate praise. They weren't playing a game or manipulating Sean. They saw he was not only clever, but he was also kind. They saw and acknowledged how he helped others. Many found the outdoors very uncomfortable, even miserable. Not so, Sean. He helped others adapt.

Finally, weeks later than initially anticipated, Sean started to open up. He eventually shared his own story. And the others helped him to begin to see though his own façade. They helped him to see how he was deceiving himself in the way that he thought about his life and his problems.

Even as they held him up to the truth of the mirror when it came to his alcohol and drugs, they also held him up to the same mirror of truth when it came to his talents, strength, and abilities. He was being surrounded by candor.

Sean was starting, for the first time since as far back as 5th grade, to see some of the truths he preferred to deny.

Sure he had dyslexia, but what was so bad about that, particularly when compared to what some of the other's faced.

And Attention Deficit Disorder? Others had it, acknowledged it, and faced it. And they seemed to be OK. He wouldn't self-destruct by acknowledging his diagnosis.

Why did he have to drink?

Why did he have to cop an attitude?

Why was he causing himself so much difficulty?

Why was he unwilling to accept that he had alcoholism?

The process of facing interior demons was beginning.

Chapter 8 -- WHAT NEXT?

The wilderness program was designed to get the individual to open up, to admit he or she had a problem. For, until problems are acknowledged, there is no way they will be faced.

None of us is going to accept responsibility for problems we deny.

On the other hand, just because we have come to see a problem doesn't mean we are ready to accept responsibility for that problem -- particularly if we don't hold ourselves in very high esteem.

Sean had, reluctantly, come to admit he had some problems. However, he was not so sure he wanted to accept responsibility for those problems. His self-image wasn't strong enough. He was like many others who go through such programs, and many of us who don't. He was just beginning his journey of recovery.

The next step was to be in another program. A program where one could stabilize. In Sean's case he needed to stabilize his sobriety -- and to begin to practice behaviors that would lead to sustained resolve. Eventually, from an internal "place" of resolve, one could begin to develop the skills needed to live life productively – in Sean's case as a sober and responsible person. And to be able to do so without continued need of a "program".

Sean had taken a number of weeks longer than most to open up. Now there was a push to find a suitable secondary program for Sean. His next step, if you will.

Each additional day Sean spent in Second Nature, however, meant more decisions and more money ($495 per day) from your Granddad.

This whole period, from the origin of the idea to help Sean, in December, until the end of March was a massively difficult time for his Dad. Financially and emotionally.

Financially he had more and more money going out. Much faster than he could ever make such money. And, it was being spent in quantities he found hard to believe.

Emotionally there was no one to "go through" this with. If he had had the support of Sean's mother in any form it would have made a big difference for him. He felt so alone. Essentially, she had abandoned him. But that actually happened years before, Mariah. Despite that past however, he continued to hope somehow she might see how much he was trying to help Sean and offer, at least, encouragement. None came. Not even understanding. And she continued to make it clear any financial help from her was out of the question. She missed an opportunity for so much good. She chose the opposite. She was consistent; she made it very clear she opposed this help for Sean.

As the next program was being considered, Sean offered a surprisingly honest and considerate insight. He acknowledged that if the next program was within walking distance of a drinking establishment then he was virtually certain that as soon as he became stressed, he would simply walk out the door and head for the booze. And he knew such behavior would lead to his dismissal from any program and that would "waste all the money his Dad had spent on him."

This was seen, paradoxically, as a sign of thoughtfulness. A sign of improvement.

Both the educational consultant and your Grandfather hoped Sean would go on with his education as part of the next program. But Sean was not the least bit interested. He still hated the thought of school. Mariah, you will better be able to understand Sean's strong distaste for school as this story goes on.

Sean wanted a program where he could be outside and outdoors. But, doing what?

The idea of organic farming came up and a program called STRAIGHT ARROW was introduced. It was in northern Washington State, near the Canadian border. It was run by Bruce Morelli and his wife, Shirley. Unfortunately, it offered no formal therapy. Just hard work, in a "clean" (alcohol and drug free) supportive environment.

Sean liked the thought of organic farming. He was not the least bit interested in "therapy." This program was far away from temptation. Sean would consider it, but he was still afraid.

He wanted to check it out, before he committed. And they wanted to check him out, before they committed.

This next step was to be no easier than the first step.

It is important to remember, he was still under the authority of the court. And, he was also an adult who legally could choose for himself – whether to go into a program or back to detention. The court had to agree. And Sean had to commit.

How to get Sean up to Washington State and the program? Fortunately a counselor with Second Nature, the wilderness program, was willing to accompany Sean (for an added fee). Sean couldn't be allowed to go alone.

Sean further complicated things by wanting to go back to Albuquerque for a day. He was still more interested in the legal matters (outside of himself) than in making his own changes (inside of himself).

Eventually he made it up there, but the matter was far from settled. His chaperone left Sean with the Morellis. They didn't just run the program, they were the program.

As soon as Sean arrived, the jousting for power and control started. Sean wanted some things his way. And Bruce wouldn't agree to have Sean on board without a genuine commitment from Sean. Sean balked.

Meanwhile, your Granddad, hoping all would go well, left for southern New Mexico to help a friend. He was in Silver City when Bruce called and told him Sean was leaving. Another crisis.

Bruce dropped Sean off on the state road several miles away from the rural farm. Sean had only a few bucks in his pocket. My friend knew what Sean would do. He would immediately call his mom, and after he explained his situation, she would rescue him. Somehow she would get him back to New Mexico.

The cycle that had started years earlier was repeating itself. He was going to run away from his responsibilities, and do it with the help of his mother. His Father had to try to stop that.

Your Grandfather immediately called Louella, trying to reach her before Sean did. He explained what was happening and what Sean was facing. He explained that if no one rescued Sean then he might turn around and go back and accept the terms Bruce Morelli was proposing.

She didn't seem to think Sean had to go back to Straight Arrow if he didn't want to do so. She didn't seem to grasp the limited options available to Sean. If Sean returned to New Mexico, what were his options? Your Granddad walked her through the logic and asked for her support. She balked. He pleaded. The cycle repeated. His Dad could only help Sean if his mother agreed to cooperate. She held all the power.

This was the craziness that happens in a dysfunctional family.

Louella wasn't willing to admit Sean needed help. She refused to see clearly or to acknowledge fully and openly the breadth and severity of the problems he was facing. Your Grandfather, even though he knew and understood what help was needed, had little if any influence over Sean. It was, as I told you, crazy. Despite her lack of insight, she held the power.

How could this be? Why was this happening?

Sean needed someone to help him if he was going to continue living as he was – irresponsibly. And, as long as his life was enmeshed with hers, as long as she supported him then he could easily continue his drinking and drug use. She had power and influence over him. He needed her, because without her help he would have had to face the consequences of his own decisions. With her help, he could avoid those consequences, and deny his problems.

With continued pleading by your Grandfather, Louella agreed (a) to not help Sean get back to New Mexico and (b) to tell him to return to Straight Arrow.

Sure enough, as Grandpa expected, it was only minutes after their phone call was over when Sean reached her by phone. Fortunately, she kept her word. She would not send money for his return and she told him to return to Straight Arrow.

Not surprisingly, Sean was not so ready to listen, even to his enabler. He balked. Over the next few hours, on the side of the road in rural Washington, he considered his options. Eventually, with no one to rescue him from the consequences of his decision to leave Straight Arrow, he decided to go back.

The problem now was: Would the Morellis accept him back?

Sean didn't want to call and ask Bruce Morelli to take him back as that would mean he had to humble himself and ask for help, to admit his need for the Morellis' help. They would win the power struggle.

Sean found his cell phone battery was running down. He had limited calls and needed to make a decision. Eventually, with Louella's encouragement, Sean called his Dad. Your Granddad recommended Sean call Bruce Morelli and ask to be allowed to return. Sean still balked. Sean was having to deal with consequences and having to face his need for help. And, to be clear, Sean was afraid.

To return to Straight Arrow would mean Sean had to accept responsibility for his problem. And your Granddad told me that he thought Sean was afraid he would fail. Sean had come to accept he had a drinking and drug problem, but he was not so sure he wanted to give them up. Better than anyone, he knew the power they had over him, and he lacked confidence in his ability to overcome that power.

To his credit, your Dad finally did call Bruce Morelli. While reluctant, he agreed to Mr. Morelli's terms, all except one. He would not cut his hair.

The Morellis agreed to accept him back.

But by now it was already late in the day. The Morellis were not going to hop in their vehicle and go get him. They told him to fend for himself for the night, and that he could get himself back to the farm the next day. More consequences for him to face.

He had never really had to fend for himself. He always had others to fall back on. He wasn't really as tough and independent as he imagined himself to be. (Unfortunately, he never completely gave up that self-image. It would play a role in his death.)

With some suggestions by Mr. Morelli and telephone guidance by his parents, he found his way down the country road and with the little money he had left he got a room for the night. He had never had to do that kind of thing by himself before.

Then he had to spend the night mentally reviewing the day, his predicament, his decisions, and his future. By your Granddad's recollection, Sean had a beer or two that night, too. But it is now years later and my friend really couldn't remember with certainty.

The next day, Sean made it back to Straight Arrow.

Chapter 9 -- ORGANIC FARMING AND SOBRIETY

What was Straight Arrow like?

Your Grandfather never got to see the place. He had to spend his time working, to generate money to pay the $6,000 per month bill. But he never got a chance to see the farm and the surrounding area.

What he did come to understand about Straight Arrow was that the Morellis created a homey atmosphere on a multi-thousand acre place. He remembered Sean telling him that from one spot on or near the farm one could look down on Canada, it was that close to the border.

There were a number of crops being grown and lots of work to juggle. Trees to tend, planting in the spring, and I believe there was green house work too. Sean told his Dad how it was common place to see native animals, such as deer, elk, moose, and even bears.

However, there was no therapy. So, Sean was gaining no conscious insight into his problems.

What he did get was time away from alcohol and drugs.

It seems your Dad thrived up there. He loved being outdoors and he was energized by being productive.

When it came to work, Sean was a model. Indeed, your Grandfather learned Sean would cajole and prod other young men (the place didn't take on any women clients) to get up and work hard. And when they didn't, it seems, he shamed them into doing their share.

Sean's hard work and the quality of his work were noticed. That led to him being assigned by Mr. Morelli to some more-skilled tasks. I believe he supervised some of the outdoor projects for Mr. Morelli and he was assigned to some "inside work" of painting and remodeling. If your Granddad's memory is correct, that was work actually done inside of the Morelli's home.

Sean started there on March 27, 2008.

Just as he had at the wilderness program, so too at Straight Arrow, Sean received genuine positive feedback and praise for hard work.

When had he last had consistent praise for good choices? How long had it been since he was making good choices consistently?

His Father thinks the last time Sean had made good choices with any degree of regularity -- and thus received regular legitimate and genuine praise -- had been in grade school!!!

How hard it must have been for Sean all those years in between?

At one level or another he must have known that his choices all those years were not "good" ones. Now that he was alcohol and drug free, he was making good choices. A positive cycle of reinforcement had replaced a negative cycle.

Mariah, I have shared with you, so far, but one period of your Father's life. I must continue and share more of his life for you to fully understand the thoughts and the emotions that tore through my friend that day after your Dad died.

By knowing more of your Dad's life and then by understanding what your Granddad experienced that day, you will better be able to understand why your Grandfather believed your Dad didn't have to die.

Sean's earliest years seemed joyful, according to his Father. Your Granddad did everything he could to make sure Sean was with him whenever he was home. He fondly remembers frequently carrying Sean on his back in a "kidpack" whenever he could: working on ditches, irrigating the land, building the addition to the house. He specifically recalls teaching Sean how to say new sounds, letters, and words. But there was not much time for such closeness as your Grandfather was working as a doctor almost 85 hours a week at that time! Later his Dad had cause to wonder about Sean's experiences during those long hours while he was doing the medical work.

A few days after your father died, your Granddad found himself praying, and sobbing in pain. He missed your Dad so much.

Remember, your Dad was his little boy.

Your Granddad loved him so much that the pain was and continues to be insufferable.

As he cried his heart out in love for your Dad this particular day, he begged your Dad to know how much he loved him. What could he do, Granddad pleaded, to show his love when your Dad was no longer alive? Your Grandpa said he was startled when he sensed that Sean responded that his Dad was to "Take care of Mariah."

Of course he would.

This book is part of that commitment to care for you.

Chapter 10 -- MISTAKES

While Sean was working hard in Washington State, his Dad was working hard in Albuquerque, trying to make the money for Sean's expensive care.

It seems that Sean kept worrying about the legal problems. He kept after the Morellis about the legal situation. He kept telling them he had to get back to Albuquerque to "straighten out" the legal problems.

When asked, your Grandfather repeatedly reassured Mr. Morelli neither Sean nor he needed to worry or deal with the legal issues. My friend had a commitment from the judge that he would allow Sean as much supervised time as needed to get better.

No one knows for sure what was going on inside of Sean. But it seems he came to believe he could now control his drinking and his drug use. That he was strong enough or "well enough" to be able to be around drugs and alcohol and still be able to control his choices.

Sean's mother had consistently argued that Sean had to learn to live with his drinking. She claimed it was not necessary that he stop completely, rather he had to learn to be around alcohol, or marijuana, and simply limit his use. He needed to learn to use them responsibly – the way she did.

Louella, Sean, and the Morellis made arrangements for Louella and Maria-Teresa to go up to Washington State to see Sean. In late July, they drove all the way up.

When your Grandfather learned this was happening he was very upset. No one – not Sean, not the Morellis, and (of course) not Louella had asked your Granddad's advice about such a trip. My friend was stunned. Why would the Morellis agree to Louella's visit when she had done nothing to help him get care? What was going through their minds? She had not sacrificed a penny to help Sean. She had tried to keep Sean from getting help. How was her visit going to be a good thing for Sean?

Once it was clear the trip was going to occur, your Grandfather warned Bruce Morelli to be careful. He made it very clear to the Morellis that Louella was a big part of Sean's problems. He reminded them Sean had been under her roof for four years and had nothing to show for that time. He reminded Bruce Morelli that Sean got into his legal trouble under her guidance. He reminded them she had refused to get involved in the therapy provided by the wilderness program, Second Nature. He told them how she had refused to read about, to learn about, and to understand her role in Sean's problems.

My friend had learned about his role in Sean's problems from the wilderness program. They offered wonderful help and information and resources for the families of the young people enrolled. Your Granddad had come to see clearly the dysfunctional interactions of the family that made it impossible for Sean to successfully deal with his problems.

Louella, on the other hand, had refused to take the therapy and refused to look at her role in Sean's difficulties.

Let me share with you what he learned, and what Louella did not learn. (And there is more information available on this if you would like to understand better – see Section II.)

Your Grandfather was self-disciplined. He could be firm. He expected his son to grow up and become self-disciplined.

Louella was a free spirit and fun loving. Anything that made her life more difficult she avoided if she could.

When Sean would come up against challenges, his Father would push and encourage Sean (a) to accept the issue or problem and (b) to see that he (Sean) had the power to deal with it and to work through it.

When Louella saw Sean struggling to "work through" an issue, she would take compassion on him. She would try to protect Sean from the pain of the struggle. And she would undermine the process (of growth) and help him find a way out of the painful toil.

The more she interfered with Sean's growth the more upset your Grandfather became with her. He would repeatedly try to teach her and show her how she was actually hurting Sean. She refused to accept what Granddad was explaining to her.

The cycle was clear. The more she was "soft" the more he would become "hard". This was one of the classic family dynamics that was clearly described by the therapeutic program at Second Nature.

Sean's Father was "firm and harsh". Sean's mother was "kind and sweet". Sean would consistently choose "kind and sweet". Who wouldn't?

Problem: Sean's choices got him into more and more bad decisions. And the consequences got bigger and bigger.

When he got into big problems, then Louella or Sean would come to his Dad. And his Dad would figure out a way to help him. Then Granddad would tell Sean not to do it again. And Granddad would hope Sean had learned his lesson.

Wrong !!! Wrong thing to do.

Your Dad was said to have the problem (in this case with alcohol and drugs) but, in reality, the "problem" was a family problem. The family unit was broken.

Sean had an "enabler" for a mother. And he had a "rescuer" for a father.

His father and mother were a big part of Sean's problems. They were not a team. They were not united, and had not been for years. There was no leader. There was no "head of the house".

Sean was trapped with his problems in a household that made it worse for him, not better.

Think about it. Any child would pick "kind and sweet" over "firm and harsh". Any of us, when young, would make the same choices he did.

Because of the difference between his parents, Sean had not been allowed to learn. He had been constantly rescued from the steady stream of challenges and issues; he was rescued from the steady stream of painful consequences that give a young person the opportunity to learn. He had not been allowed to develop the self-confidence that comes from successfully struggling. Without that experience and without that self-confidence, how was he to face the bigger and bigger issues and challenges that come with growing up? He hadn't been allowed to develop the self-discipline that is required for maturation. His maturation had been arrested.

When Louella and Maria-Teresa arrived at Straight Arrow, the Morellis allowed them to take Sean on a "road trip" to the surrounding areas. I am sure they had a great time. Sean would have been very happy to see them. And they Sean.

Over those several days Sean readily convinced Louella he had to get back to Albuquerque to clear up his legal problems.

They never consulted my friend. Louella had had nothing to do with the judge or the court. They didn't know what they were even taking about. AND THEY DIDN'T WANT TO KNOW, as you will see.

They got back to the farm and they discussed their plan with the Morellis. The Morellis didn't bother to call your

Granddad. The Morellis made a BIG MISTAKE. The Morellis allowed themselves to be manipulated. They agreed to let Sean go back to Albuquerque to deal with the legal issues, with a promise from Louella that she would bring Sean right back. And then the Morellis waited to call and tell his Father AFTER Louella, Sean, and Maria-Teresa had left!!! They didn't even have the decency to ask your Grandfather about the decision.

Your Grandfather was furious. He had worked so hard to get Sean this help. And he knew what was going to happen. And it did.

The Morellis, to this day, have never apologized (a) for deceiving and cheating your Granddad, (b) for allowing themselves to be manipulated by an alcoholic liar and his enabling mother, and (c) for misguiding Sean. They were supposed to be knowledgeable about alcoholism. They had been warned. My friend had told them not to trust Louella. They should have known better than to let Sean leave as they did.

Chapter 11 -- BACK TO THE SAME

Sean got back to Albuquerque. The judge saw the good progress that Sean had made. The judge saw that Sean was "clean." Sean was allowed to go free.

However, he did not return to Straight Arrow as he had promised the Morellis. Louella did not force him to return to Straight Arrow as she promised the Morellis.

Sean resumed living with Louella.

He resumed drinking. He resumed drugs. Louella continued to enable him. Just as before. She provided him a home, food, a cellular phone. She allowed him to use the money he earned from odd jobs on cigarettes, alcohol, and drugs.

Your Granddad pleaded with each of them to honor their commitment, and for Sean to return to Straight Arrow. Sean needed to continue to acknowledge and care for his unresolved problems.

Your Grandfather was tormented. He called the Morellis and was told to speak only to Bruce. Shirley Morelli wanted out of the issue. He asked Bruce to call Louella and Sean and to hold them accountable. He pleaded with Mr. Morelli to try, at least verbally, to get them to honor their commitment.

Mr. Morelli refused to do even that.

What kind of man was he? He was supposed to be teaching young men to be honorable. And yet he would not even hold these two accountable.

This struck my friend as cowardice.

Your Grandfather scoured his brain trying to find a way to resume Sean's care. He no longer had the force of the court behind him. He once again became the "bad guy" in the eyes of Sean and Louella. He was the one asking and expecting each of them to behave and to make choices neither wanted any part of.

The only thing he could do was to try was to rely upon honor. The honor of a confused alcoholic son and an immature "enabling" mother.

One evening, about 3 to 6 weeks after they had come back to Albuquerque, my friend felt moved to confront them. He would do what Mr. Morelli refused to do. He would hold them accountable to their promise.

He walked the 3-4 miles from his home to the house Louella was buying. He walked instead of driving. The walk gave him time to think, to pray, to ponder, and to consider. This was the only option he had to get help to his son. He was afraid of what was going to be the outcome, but he had to try nonetheless.

There he spoke with the two of them.

He went through the sequence of events with them. Had they not told the Morellis that Sean would return? "Yes, they had made such a promise." Had the Morellis relied on both Sean's and Louella's promise to return? "Yes, they had."

Was Sean going to be a man of his word? "I am not going back." Was Sean going to be a promise keeper? "I am not going back there." Was Louella going to condone Sean's deceitful decision to stay in Albuquerque and break his promise? "I can't make him go back.".

Had Louella ever meant to keep the promise to the Morellis? "Well... " When she was making the promise to them, face-to-face at Straight Arrow, did she intend, at that moment, to keep her promise? "Not really."

Your Grandfather was stunned. Louella made it clear that deep inside, even as she said the words to the Morellis, she had intended to lie to them. She had had deceit in her heart from the beginning. Begrudgingly, she admitted it.

They smiled smugly. The two of them gloated. They had outmaneuvered your Granddad.

Neither one of them saw any reason to return. And, neither one was going to call the Morellis and so much as apologize for their failure to keep their promise.

My friend walked back home dejected. He had to accept there was nothing else he could do. He had made it clear to each of them what his values and his recommendations called for. But that was all he succeeded in doing.

Mariah, you should know some things did change for the better. Inside my friend, as he struggled in 2008 to help Sean, he had come to see more clearly his own role in the dysfunctional family. And he knew he could no longer play into the dysfunction. He would no longer be the "rescuer."

And, he no longer felt the deep guilt and shame for failing as the head of the household.

Your Grandfather Michael no longer felt centrally responsible for Sean's failure to successfully deal with his problems.

He had taken action to correct his share of the problems. He knew Sean now had enough insight to choose his own path. And he knew with certainty that Sean's mother had been given opportunity to grow and become Sean's adult mother rather than continuing and acting as his adolescent friend.

They both had been given a chance to participate in a solution.

For now, while he feared for his son, he had a partial sense of peace for having planted the seed of insight within Sean.

Settled back in Albuquerque, Sean and Louella went "Back-to-the-Same."

Sixteen months of "Back-to-the-Same" and Sean was still without a driver's license, without a stable job, without an education. He was doing drugs with his alcohol. And he was irresponsibly having sex, including messing around with your mother.

Your Grandfather was kept out of the picture. They did not share with him. They would not share with him because they knew your Grandfather would not have approved. My friend was seen as the problem.

Later, your Grandfather learned your mother and father had actually lived with Louella. It was about the time you were conceived. And that is why they, and your mother's mother, Cynthia, assumed that you were Sean's child.

It never made sense to your Grandfather how Louella could consider herself to be a good Catholic and a good Christian, yet she was breaking the rules of a God she claimed to love and honor. She was not only condoning, but she was helping her son to continue to do the wrong things. Including, in this case, living with someone out of wedlock, in her home.

Chapter 12 -- THE NEXT CRISIS

During the 16 months or so after your Dad left Straight
Arrow, his Father saw very little of Sean.

Sean knew his Dad did not agree with Sean's choices and
his chosen ways of spending his life.

And my friend knew Sean was not going to listen to any
significant suggestions he made.

Your Granddad saw how Sean was wasting his life. And,
despite his love for Sean, he could do nothing.

One of the books he had read, I believe he received it from
Maria-Teresa, *The Lost Years* by Constance Curry and
Kristina Wandzilak, was written by an alcoholic and her
mother. It explained how there is virtually nothing the
loving family can do for the alcoholic, when they do not
want help.

It was a terrible time for my friend. Knowing his son was
wasting away and there was nothing he could do about it.

Then one day in December, 2009, your Grandfather got a
call from Louella. Could she talk to him?

Yes.

She explained how Sean was again in the county detention center. How he had been on probation for a 3rd DWI. And how he got himself into even more trouble.

Granddad asked for some details.

The night of his most recent arrest, Louella said, she had gone with Sean to a party of a friend of hers. She and Sean drank at the party. They went back to her rental (she had been unable to keep up the house payments and had moved to a rental). She had to go to work the next day, so she went to bed. Sean had stayed up. She assumed he was going to just watch TV.

She said that the next thing she knew the police were knocking at her door.

Apparently Sean had left the place, taken her car, and gone out. She didn't know where or when or with whom. His driving must have caught the attention of police. With the police on his tail, he sped home and ran inside. They followed him. When they accused him, he claimed he was not the driver of the vehicle.

Sean was apparently petrified. He was already on probation. He knew if he got into any more legal trouble, the punishment would be harsh.

So he lied.

The police didn't believe him. They arrested him. They charged him with another DWI.

Sean's poor judgment had continued.

And so had his mother's.

What could she have been thinking? Her son was an alcoholic. He had repeatedly demonstrated that when he drank he couldn't stop drinking. He couldn't stop drinking until he was drunk. And when he got drunk his judgment was all messed up. He would make horrible decisions and take inappropriate risks.

She knew that.

Yet she took him with her to where he would most surely drink alcohol.

What kind of thinking is that? What kind of love is that? What kind of choice is that?

She explained to his Dad she didn't know what to do, to help Sean.

He responded by asking her why she had called him.

She repeated she did not know what to do. Sean was now facing a fourth degree felony.

He reminded her she had caused the problem by "rescuing" Sean from the treatment program 16 months earlier. He reminded her that she surely knew there were going to be consequences to that choice. She must have known a recurrence – just like the one Sean was now facing -- was likely, given Sean's failure to continue treatment.

Why should he do anything?

She again pleaded she did not know what to do. Sean could be sentenced to time in prison.

He told her she should take responsibility for her actions and her decisions. He told her she should help Sean, as she was the one who had led him away from solutions and back to mistakes.

She repeated: she did not know what to do.

He would think about it, but she was not to expect anything from him.

He thought for several days.

What to do?

He had very mixed feelings. And competing thoughts. Part of him didn't care -- this time -- that Sean was sitting in a detention center. Sean had made decisions. Sean surely knew there would be consequences to those decisions.

After what he had learned when Sean was last in treatment, your Grandfather had promised himself that he would not repeat the cycle. He would no longer be the rescuer.

What should he do? What could he do?

Clearly, Louella was a major part of Sean's problem. The two were enmeshed. If she didn't change it would be very hard, if not impossible, for Sean to really change. She was Sean's enabler.

Your Grandfather knew she COULD change. He had seen others change.

But WOULD she?

He had to hope.

What would happen if he didn't try.

They could each change – Sean and Louella. They could both change -- Sean and Louella.

He hoped they could.   He hoped they would.

He had to hope.

He decided to help, if...
- If they both agreed to change, to fully participate in whatever program was given them,
- If they both agreed to participate in paying for the services, and,
- If they both understood that your Granddad would never rescue Sean again.

He met with Louella. He asked her if she would commit herself to change. He asked if she would take advantage of the therapy that would be made available to her. If she would look deeply inside, and examine her role in Sean's cycle of problems. He asked if she would change, and stop her behaviors that allowed Sean to continue with his unhealthy and dangerous choices.

She considered.

She agreed.

He then asked if she would be willing to pay, to sacrifice her own money, to help Sean.

She balked. She claimed she had no savings.

My friend was not surprised. He had already anticipated this. He had watched her, over the years. She would consistently spend more money than she made. He had repeatedly bailed her out financially. That had been part of what drove them apart.

Fortunately, his problem-solving mind had seen a way around her lack of funds, and in a manner that could benefit both Sean and Louella -- if they kept their word.

He proposed that she and Sean take out a joint loan. However, as neither she nor Sean had any credit or collateral, Granddad said he would arrange for the loan. Then, when they paid off the loan they would each have improved credit.

She agreed.

He made it very clear to her that he would NEVER rescue Sean again. If this attempt to help Sean failed, then Sean would face future consequences without any help from his Father.

She stated she understood.

Now, to meet with Sean.

Chapter 13 -- WAITING TO TALK TO SEAN

To meet with Sean, your Granddad had to go to the
Bernalillo County Detention Center.

My friend had never imagined that he would ever have to
see one of his children behind bars. And yet he had already
had to deal with Sean being locked up four times. The
thought of having to again go to the county detention
center, wait for hours, and then see his son through a closed
circuit video connection was, as it always was, emotionally
painful.

What gave him strength this time was the hope Sean could
once again get onto a path of healing.

Before leaving for the detention center he had to go on-line.
There he found out what pod or area Sean was being
"housed" in. Then he could determine the visiting hours
for that particular pod. He made arrangements to be off
work at the right time.

When the time came, he drove over, went in, and signed in.
Then he had to sit with the other people who were waiting
to see one of their family members who was locked up.
The wait would be hours.

As he sat there, he thought of all the opportunity Sean had
had for such a different life, a better life. He thought of all
the stupid and foolish and mean things Sean's mother had
done.

He thought of how Sean had been dealt a very rough set of cards (to use the card player's analogy): dyslexia, attention deficit disorder, and alcoholism.

He was certain, as a physician, that every one of those problems was treatable and Sean could have overcome them.

He knew God had, over time, led others -- helpers and healers – to learn about and develop ways to treat and to help fellow humans who got dealt each of those challenges. Indeed, your Grandfather had worked with patients and families with each of those problems. He had seen how strong parents, who were willing and able to sacrifice, demonstrated over and over what miracles are made of. He saw the children who reached their maximum and their potential through the loving sacrifice of others.

He had witnessed this even in his own family. His older brother and his wife had shown what loving sacrifice could do. Their son, Sean's cousin, Mark, had autism. That problem, while different, was at least as big a challenge as any of Sean's issues. Yet, unlike Sean, every time Granddad saw Mark, Mark was improving. Over the previous 20 years, my friend would see Mark every 4 to 6 months, on average. And, every time, Sean's Dad would notice how Mark had advanced.

Why was Mark consistently improving and Sean consistently going nowhere? Or doing worse? What was fundamentally different in Mark's life from Sean's?

Your Grandfather realized Sean had a fourth problem that Mark did not have. Sean had a parent who had a very different attitude toward life, and a very different attitude toward the kind of problems Sean was born with. His mother was a "fatalist." She grew up a "fatalist."

What does that mean, to be a fatalist? Well, it means we are to accept our fate. We are to accept the way we are created. Who are we to think we can change what God has created?

Don't expect a fatalist to tell you they are a fatalist. They have probably never even heard the word. But through their understanding of life and/or their understanding of creation and of God, they believe we humans are to accept ourselves and each other as we are.

Fatalists are uncomfortable with "labeling" someone. If someone is different, it is not "right" to put a label on that person. We are to love one another, we are to love them as God created them. Labeling a person is like calling a person a "bad name." Labeling is blaming. Who are we to blame or complain? We are mere humans. We are to accept God's will. God's will is fate.

And that fourth problem, your Grandfather was NEVER able to solve. All the way to the end of Sean's life that fourth problem continued.

Sitting there at the detention center, waiting for someone else's permission to see his own son, my friend had a lot of time to think.

He thought about all the different ways he had tried to get Sean's mother to become a strong, mature, guide for Sean, rather than Sean's friend and, later, Sean's drinking partner. He thought about how he must have made mistakes or else she would have changed. He loved her, but he hated what she would do – and what she would not do.

That day, like so many others, was very painful and difficult for Sean's Dad. His heart was broken. Despite his realization 16 months earlier, he felt, once again, he had failed as the head of the household. He had never been able to get Sean's mother to fully accept the diagnosis and/or treatment of Sean's three problems.

Oh, she would say the words and carry out some actions to deal with some of the problems. But she never demonstrated a positive, joyful, optimistic, "can-do" attitude that would inspire Sean to self confidence and self-esteem. She acted as if Sean's "being labeled" was hurtful to Sean – and/or, dishonorable to her and to her family.

He, your Granddad, saw things very differently. To his way of thinking, "labels" – the naming of Sean's problems -- were opportunities. A label was an opportunity to see, to know, to understand, and to deal with the underlying problem. Sean's labels of Dyslexia, of Attention Deficit Disorder, and, now, of Alcoholism were empowerment.

A diagnosis was a ticket to the solution. A diagnosis was the path to learning from all of the other helpers and healers who had shared solutions to the problem.

For Grandfather Michael, Sean was not the "problem." Sean was a wonderful miracle of God's creation who had a problem or problems.

To his thinking, it was "how the problem was faced" that determined one's character. Not the fact of the problem itself.

Your Grandfather had come to fully understand the consequences of this failure – the failure of he and Sean's mother to unite with a pro-active attitude and a pro-active approach to Sean's problems. Sean had been left floating aimlessly through life by that failure. The aimless floating led to Sean's making mistake after mistake.

Fortunately, Grandpa also had hope that day. It wasn't all regrets.

My friend knew Sean needed to be around those who could guide him and teach him. Around those who could be good strong examples and role models. Sean needed more time sober and doing good things for which he would get sincere and honest feedback that was positive. He needed to get back on the positive cycle. He needed to get back onto the positive cycle that his mother had "rescued" him from when she took him from Straight Arrow.

It seemed to your Grandfather that God was giving all three of them another chance.

Chapter 14 -- SEAN'S COMMITMENT, AND A PLAN

Finally, the waiting was over.

Granddad was led from the waiting room to a room full of closed circuit monitors. He was given a number and told to have a seat in front of the monitor with the corresponding number. He was to put on the earphones, and to wait for his son to appear.

Shortly, Sean appeared on the screen. He was dressed in an orange "jumpsuit" – the same as every other inmate.

A few superficial greetings were passed. It was awkward. Your Dad and his father were, as I explained, estranged from one another. They had had little contact since Sean quit the Straight Arrow program in Washington State.

He asked Sean his version of why he was locked up once again. Sean whitewashed the story. He put the kind of spin on it that might help if it went to court. Sean was not being fully truthful – something he had been taught by his mother. My friend could guess what had really happened. And he decided it would do no good to press Sean, at that time, to confess.

Granddad explained to Sean how Louella had asked for his help. He asked Sean if he wanted his help. Sean said he did.

Your Grandfather then laid out the offer.

Granddad would put out his time and energy to help.

Granddad would pay for treatment/therapy.

If Sean would:

a.) Agree to fully participate in any therapy that could be arranged;

b.) Help pay off a loan taken out to pay for legal expenses;

c.) Understand and accept that his Father would NEVER rescue him again.

Sean asked a few questions about details. Then he committed.

Your Grandfather thought Sean really was truthful in his commitments. But how could he know for sure as Sean had become a very effective, manipulative liar. He wouldn't know for sure until it came to witnessing Sean's actions.

With the agreements, Sean's Dad went to work on all that had to be arranged. A therapeutic plan had to be developed. A lawyer had to be hired. And a loan had to be arranged.

Louella didn't know how to do any of these things and never offered to learn or to help.

That day, after meeting with Sean, he started by calling Kim Rubin, the educational consultant in Santa Fe who had helped Sean get his first chance two years earlier. Ms. Rubin listened intently to what had happened over the past 16 months, and all about Sean's present legal problem. Then she told Granddad she had sold her business.

He was stunned and afraid of what that would mean. He didn't have other options or time to consider other possibilities. Fortunately, Ms. Rubin told him how to reach the new owner and recommended her highly . And she promised to call ahead and brief the new owner on Sean's situation. He was surprised the new owner lived in New York City.

Her name was Cynthia Cohen and she turned out to be very kind, very understanding, and very competent.

A day or so later the two of them talked in more detail. She offered a discount for her services because there was already a record on Sean. And she did this despite the fact she herself was not familiar with Sean's history.

Your Grandfather Michael was surprised that she wanted to come to Albuquerque and to meet and to talk individually and personally with him, and with Sean, and with Louella. He worried about the added cost. She assured him she would be reasonable. And she was.

Through a friend of his he had met a lawyer who specialized in DWI cases. He called and presented the circumstances. Mr. Preciado agreed to represent Sean. Of course, he couldn't promise anything. But he would do his best. They discussed the payment arrangements. He would need $1000 to get started. My friend agreed to get him a check while the loan was being set up for Sean and Louella.

Then he went to the credit union. He met with the manager. He described how he was willing to deposit money as collateral for the loan to Louella and Sean. They would be fully and legally responsible to pay the loan back.

And, as he had promised, their credit would be improved when that was completed.

Unfortunately, when it became clear to Mr. Preciado that Sean actually had two legal (DWI) cases, his fee increased and within weeks the loan had to be increased. Granddad again made those arrangements with and for Sean and his mother, after each agreed to the additional amount.

Each of the pieces needed for Sean to have another chance to learn, to grow, and to free himself of the power of his alcohol and drug addiction were in place. Each person had to follow through on his or her commitment for this to become reality.

Chapter 15 -- MAYBE A SECOND CHANCE FOR SEAN

The next few weeks were full of action.

Your Granddad made a return trip to the detention center to inform Sean of the arrangements. As before, it was full of pain and required patience.

Mr. Preciado would meet with Sean. He would also meet with Louella, as she was a witness to some of the events leading to the latest charges against Sean.

Louella would sign for the loan. Sean would have to do so later, as he was still in detention.

Louella got Mr. Preciado paid from the loan proceeds. Your Grandfather would eventually get his $1000 down payment reimbursed.

Mr. Preciado was placed in touch with Ms. Cohen.

Ms. Cohen did, indeed, come to Albuquerque. She spent several days. She met with each person involved. She was able to get into the detention center to meet with Sean face-to-face. This was made possible through special permission obtained by Mr. Preciado, as non-family members were not normally allowed to visit detainees.

Everyone was working hard. Sean was very fortunate.
But…

What would the judges decide?

Would Sean follow through with his commitments?

Would Louella follow through, and keep her commitments?

There was a great deal at stake. Sean's future depended on
a lot of things going well.

Ms. Cohen quickly concluded that Sean's chances of long-
term sobriety were slim without therapy. The likelihood of
Sean staying sober required that he have more experience
living sober and a supportive alcohol, drug-free
environment. But more importantly, in the long-term, Sean
needed therapy. He needed to understand the nature of
addiction and the nature of his own psyche. He had been to
meeting after meeting with Alcoholics Anonymous without
significant change in attitude or in behavior.

His chances of long-term success would also depend a
great deal on the ability of his mother to change. Would
she be able to help and support him, or would she remain
enmeshed and continue to enable his addictive behavior?
If Sean went to a therapeutic program, such a program
would offer her education and support as well. That would
make it easier for her to keep her commitment to learn
about alcoholism and to change her role in Sean's
addictions.

In addition Ms. Cohen also came to believe Sean could be successfully encouraged and supported in pursuing higher education. This was a pleasant surprise and "extra" for your Grandfather. He had been unsuccessfully trying to make this argument to Sean for so long he had almost given up on the idea of Sean getting a higher education.

In Ms. Cohen, you're my friend finally felt he had a strong ally and partner. She was advocating not only for a path to sobriety for Sean, but also for his mental health, his maturation, and a future that could be positive and fruitful.

She recommended a different wilderness program than the one your Dad had attended two years earlier. This new one, called Aspiro, had a therapeutic component she thought was deeper and more insightful. This recommendation was to be very positive for Sean. Her knowledge about this program, as opposed to others, was invaluable. Your Granddad knew he would never have been able to see those program differences without her help.

She used her expertise, and all the information available to her, including all the detailed history that which your Grandfather had sent to Ms. Rubin two years earlier, to coordinate among the lawyer, the program, Sean, and his parents.

The legal situation was not so straight forward as it was two years earlier. If Sean was to be given permission to go for help this time, there were two charges and two cases to consider, and two courts and two judges to convince.

Mr. Preciado, the lawyer, believed that if the judge who had jurisdiction over Sean for the 3rd DWI, the case for which he had been on probation, would agree to allow Sean to go (while still under her jurisdiction), then the second judge, before whom Sean was not yet convicted of the 4th DWI charge, would most likely agree (while still remaining under her jurisdiction as well).

Either and both of the judges would be more inclined to allow Sean to go for help and therapy if the prosecuting attorney(s) would agree. And it became confusing as to which jurisdiction had prosecuting authority and responsibility in Sean's second case.

You can see that this whole process, of trying to get help for Sean, was tricky and delicate and expensive.

Sean was very fortunate to get the help that he did.

Everyone prepared.

Finally, a court date was set to present the plan to the first judge, Judge Rogers.

Louella and Granddad sat there as if united, for the judge. But were they?

Unfortunately, Mariah, as you will see, the discord would continue to the end. And this discord between Sean's parents was probably the biggest mistake of all.

Chapter 16 -- TWO DIFFERENT PEOPLE

All of them arrived early.

There were other cases to precede Sean's.

There was waiting. Once again, waiting.

Your Grandfather sat there, next to Louella. They were both there to support Sean. If only they had joined together in supporting Sean years ago, he thought. What a different life Sean would have had?

Sean grew up with two parents in conflict.

My friend thought back to when this first became obvious to him.

Like any two people, they were different. When they first married, my friend thought the differences were minor and superficial. It turned out they were major and fundamental.

They came from different backgrounds. Louella was raised rural and provincial. Granddad had been raised urban and educated.

But they were both raised Catholic. Granddad assumed from their common religious beliefs they would have similar values.

Your great-Grandfather Hennelly, your Granddad's father, had grown up in rural Ireland. My friend was, thus, only one generation removed from a rural background. And, he had chosen to go to the semi-rural town of Espanola, New Mexico, expecting what he thought of as "small-town values." (He buffered that decision by being close to the nearby cities of Santa Fe and Los Alamos.) Thus, early in the relationship, he didn't think Louella's background was going to be a major source of difference from his.

It was not until your Dad was diagnosed with dyslexia that my friend began to realize what a profound -- and for him bizarre –difference there was.

With that diagnosis of Sean, my friend was about to learn that he and Louella had markedly different approaches and attitudes toward dealing with life's challenges. This disparity was to be a major source of tragedy in Sean's life.

Mariah, before I go on, let me share something your Grandfather wanted me to be sure to write down for you. Your Granddad didn't know if someday you (or, maybe, one of your children) would be affected by any of the challenges that your Dad wrestled with. But if you were to be so affected (by dyslexia or ADD or addiction or maybe even something else), he desperately wanted you to avoid the unnecessary pain and suffering that your Dad had experienced.

Your Dad's dyslexia wasn't diagnosed until just before he started the fifth grade. But when Sean was in second grade he had showed signs of trouble with reading. My doctor friend suspected then that he might have dyslexia.

Why was he suspicious?

He had many reasons.

You see, when Sean's Dad and Louella were dating, he had learned how Louella's father had trouble reading. He also learned how Louella's father had been passed over twice for promotions at his job. Your Grandfather thought that might have been due to the reading problem.

Granddad also learned that two of Louella's brothers had reading problems. One had dropped out of college. Granddad thought this brother was smart enough to have been able to get a college degree. The other brother, a talented and accomplished plumber, could never pass the test to get his plumber's license. Your Granddad, a doctor, suspected dyslexia was also behind those events.

Because of my friend's natural desire to help others, he had arranged, years before Sean was even born, for a reading teacher to work with Louella's brothers. All five had met – my friend, Louella, her two brothers, and the teacher (who was one of Grandpa's patients at his practice in Espanola). All agreed to see what could be done. Then nothing happened. Louella's brothers never showed up for the arranged help.

There was also something else that had occurred when your Dad was young. When Sean was about four years old, his Dad went up to Santa Fe and got a beginning phonics kit, to start having fun teaching Sean to read. Sean was plenty bright enough.

However, when Granddad and Sean started through the program, it was obvious that Sean was struggling.

Well, my friend was a doctor and not a teacher. So, he figured he might just have been pushing Sean into reading too soon. He set the phonics program aside.

When Sean was four and a half they moved from Espanola to Las Vegas, Nevada. Sean did fine in kindergarten and first grade. However, in second grade he showed signs of reading difficulty. The question of dyslexia came back into his Father's consideration. He arranged to have a psychologist, who was recommended by the school, test Sean. Granddad was surprised when she reported no dyslexia.

But you should know that dyslexia, at the time, was not as well understood or appreciated as it came to be a few years later. The criteria upon which to make a diagnosis were not so clear. And those with the ability to do the testing were less readily available and less well prepared. Your Granddad, who had received a wonderful education himself, had always tried to learn about lots of different things. He wanted to be able to help and direct his patients, with any kind of problems, to the best solutions possible. Dyslexia happened to be one of those problems he knew a little about.

The next year, after Sean's second grade, the family moved again. This time, from Las Vegas, Nevada, to southern California. Sean went into third grade at Our Lady of Guadalupe Parish School in La Habra. The next year, in fourth grade, as providence would have it, his teacher had a Master's Degree in Reading. About a month or so into the school year she told his parents that she thought your Dad had dyslexia. They told the teacher of the negative test results two years earlier. So, he was not then retested. However, by the end of the year there was a pattern of grades that strongly suggested dyslexia.

This time, when the teacher again suggested testing, Sean was sent. And the testing was completed during the following summer before they moved to Phoenix, where Sean would start the fifth grade.

That summer, after several days of testing, Granddad and Louella went in for the results. The doctor reported that Sean had an inherited form of dyslexia. This type, he said, it was usually mild in the girls and more marked in the boys. He then asked which others in the family had dyslexia.

Well, this was the key that unlocked the puzzle. It explained both what Sean was experiencing and what Louella's family members had experienced.

My friend was delighted to have a clear-cut diagnosis. Now they could help Sean, and help others in the family as well.

When the two of them walked out the door and down the stairs from the doctor's office your Grandfather was pleased. He expressed to Louella how happy he was to now know what the problem was. She was less than enthused. She didn't share his excitement. He didn't know why. And she didn't offer.

He would learn why, painfully, in the coming months.

Several months later, when the family went back to New Mexico for a large family gathering, my friend pulled one of his brothers-in-law aside. They went outside. My friend was excited to share the good news of Sean's diagnosis with him for two reasons. This brother-in-law was Sean's godfather, and Sean would benefit from his godfather's support as he learned to live with dyslexia. And, secondly, because this form of dyslexia was inherited, Granddad reasoned that this brother-in-law, who almost certainly had dyslexia, might have children with it, too. Granddad wanted him to be able to get help if needed. And, equally important, he could keep an eye out for the problem in other family members of the next generation. That way they too could get help if need be.

My friend thought the information was well received. He was delighted to be able to help others. And he wanted the family's support for Sean.

Unfortunately, my friend's delight was painfully naïve and short-lasting. The sharing with his brother-in-law had not been received as he had intended.

A few weeks later, back in Phoenix, after Louella received a call from her family, she pulled her husband aside. She told him that he couldn't talk to her family "that way." At first he didn't know what she meant. Then he came to realize that she meant that he could not tell her family about Sean's diagnosis of dyslexia!

He was stunned.

When he asked why he couldn't discuss Sean's dyslexia with them, she stated her brother had told their father that he was being held responsible for Sean's dyslexia. Your Grandfather blurted out that she should have corrected that misunderstanding immediately. Such a notion was absurd. Why hadn't she made it clear that no one was to blame? And that her husband was trying to help everyone.

But she hadn't.

He was astounded.

He explained again to her the genetics and how dyslexia is inherited. He reviewed what they had been told by the diagnosing doctor. He asked her to call her family back and correct the misunderstanding.

And he asked her to comprehend his thinking, as a father and as a doctor and as her husband. He was happy. Happy to have (1) a diagnosis, (2) an opportunity to help his son, and (3) the chance to potentially help members of her family. He asked her appreciation and support for his position.

He thought she came around. He could not imagine her persisting in the absurdity of the thinking that dyslexia was anybody's fault. But he was uneasy she had not taken the initiative to immediately correct the mistaken impressions in her family.

Several months later he learned the truth. They were back in New Mexico for a visit. Your Grandfather, Louella, and her parents, just the four of them, were in her parent's kitchen when Louella's father said, "So you think that it is all my fault?" He addressed the question to my friend.

Your Granddad was staggered. He turned to Louella and asked her if she had not clarified the misinformation with her family. She had not.

He asked her to do so. She would not.

She left it to your Grandfather to explain. Your Granddad told Louella's parents this was a genetic trait and that Sean's dyslexia was no more her father's fault that the color of the eyes of his children was "his fault." To a disbelieving face, he repeatedly explained dyslexia. He explained inheritance. Her parents still didn't seem to understand.

He tried a difference analogy. Diabetes. Although it is not a known genetic trait, he used this analogy of Diabetes because it was a common medical problem in Northern New Mexico. A problem he knew with certainty was familiar to her family.

Then he turned to Louella and asked again for her support in the explanation. She remained silent.

Your Granddad felt Louella was "hanging him out to dry." She was allowing her parents to remain under the false assumption my friend was humiliating her father by accusing him of causing Sean's dyslexia!

This was absurd.

This whole experience was completely bizarre and surreal for your Grandfather. This blaming had absolutely no basis in reality. He could not believe this was happening. He could not believe Louella's parents would, or even could, think he was blaming anyone. And he was paralyzed by his wife's failure to support him as her husband and as Sean's father. She refused to "set the record straight."

My friend didn't even know how to proceed further. And he felt absolutely abandoned by his own wife.

Mariah, as of my last communication with your Granddad, he told me he had no reason to believe that this illogical and erroneous understanding had ever been corrected within Louella's family.   It was only a year later, when he read a book by Malcolm Baldridge, entitled *Outliers*, that he ever found an explanation for the response of Louella and her family: HONOR.   Your Grandfather has concluded they must have felt dishonored. Nothing else ever made sense to him of this bizarre misinterpretation.

In any case, as a result of this persistent misinterpretation, her family was never open to fully accepting and embracing Sean's dyslexia.   Consequently, they never expressed any interest in his treatment or his progress, much less support.

Worse, Louella placed herself and her son, Sean, in a trap. His problem could not be openly acknowledged or discussed with her family.   To do so would bring hurt feelings to her family.

Louella left her son feeling and believing, even if never openly stating, that his dyslexia had brought pain (? dishonor) to her family.

She, consequently, left Sean with an unspeakable burden, and with no way to deal with the burden, except to be ashamed of himself. How could he ever express a feeling of shame when the topic itself was a taboo?

His Father repeatedly tried to set the record straight with and for Sean. Your Grandfather became convinced your Dad never trusted his father's attitude toward dyslexia. Why? Because he, Sean, continued to feel shame.

And that was because his mother, his other trusted window to the world, was not able to reinforce Granddad's words. Sean got mixed messages. His parents were not united.

All the way until your Father's death, this "crazy thinking" --as my friend would sometimes call it -- by Louella's family was impossible for your Grandfather to comprehend. If he had not experienced it himself, he would not have supposed people could do such an illogical thing as to assign blame for a genetic event.

It would have been simply bizarre if it were not so tragic.

And the tragedy for Sean was immense. He was never able to consciously vocalize the pain and the shame that the label of "dyslexia" caused him. But he cringed whenever it was brought up.

Paradoxically, neither Louella nor her family would ever see the pain Sean carried. To do so they would have had to accept and embrace and fully understand the problem itself.

The reality was that in fourth grade, Sean knew he had a problem. He was experiencing the problem. He knew he was not getting the spelling grades others were getting despite his best efforts. He thus concluded he was dumber than them.

In 5th grade he should have been relieved of the problem and introduced to the solution. Instead, he experienced himself as the burden. He was a defective person.

Louella's failure to support her husband, or even to trust him in this issue, drove a wedge between them that would never close.

Sean would spend many, many hours over the next five years learning to read. He succeeded.
And, this success should have bolstered his self-esteem immensely. Unfortunately, it didn't. That was because he continued to feel ashamed.

Mariah, you should know your Grandfather Michael repeatedly faulted himself as well. He wondered if it wasn't his fault for not being able to find a way to change their thinking. This continued to haunt him. I would hear him say, repeatedly, "What could I have done differently?" It was both a literal and a rhetorical question. I certainly didn't have any answers for him. Without Louella's support, how could he take on her whole family?

In any case, the two of them continued to differ fundamentally in their attitudes toward Sean's problem. And this difference would repeat itself in dealing with his other issues as well.

As a result, Sean continued to experience himself as a problem, rather than as a wonderful person with a problem.

Unfortunately, the way your Dad found to treat his shame was with alcohol and drugs.

And, the alcohol use is what led to them all being now before the court.

If they could stay united, Sean had a good chance.

Finally, the Judge was ready for Sean's hearing.

Chapter 17 -- A BIG CHANGE IN SEAN

The formalities began.

Mr. Preciado outlined the circumstances and the plan to the judge.

The prosecuting attorney expressed his reluctance.

Mr. Preciado had your Grandfather explain his support and position to the judge.

Ms. Cohen described therapeutic goals and the wilderness program to the judge.

The judge then addressed Sean, who expressed his desire for help.

Eventually, Judge Rogers became convinced Sean was not going to be a significant danger to the citizens of the State of New Mexico by being allowed to attend the supervised treatment program. She agreed to let him go there, with three stipulations.
>   (1) That he remain on probation and under her authority while gone.
>   (2) That the therapeutic programs commit to keeping her informed of his whereabouts and progress.
>   (3) That he return to court upon completion of the programs.

He could go.

A big sigh of relief.

Now for the next judge.

She saw Sean a few days later.

It turned out that Mr. Preciado's hunch was correct. The second judge did not obstruct the plan despite some opposition by the prosecuting attorney.

Sean was not free, but, rather, he was permitted to leave under the auspices of the therapeutic program, with the stipulations above. The ongoing reports would go to both judges through to a probation officer.

One more thing, your Grandfather had to put up $12,000 bail before Sean could be released.

A day later, my friend picked up his son from the detention center. They immediately left Albuquerque; it was Friday, February 12, 2010. They headed for Mount Pleasant, Utah, where Sean would begin with Aspiro -- the therapeutic, wilderness program -- the next day.

Most of the drive they respected one another's quiet. They ate munchies that had been packed for the trip. To Granddad, Sean was reflective and seemed anxious. Sean was committing to a significant change, and he knew it.

They made it to Monticello, Utah, by late afternoon where they stopped for dinner. His Dad offered to buy Sean a steak dinner. Sean loved meat. Granddad didn't have to offer twice. Sean seemed to really enjoy that meal. He hadn't had a decent meal since he entered the detention center weeks earlier.

From there they pushed on to Green River, Utah, where they spent the night. My friend remembered their night together in a small motel on the banks of the Green River. Both were a bit anxious. But both were closer. They were no longer completely estranged from one another as they had been for too many years.

The next day, they had breakfast at the motel's restaurant, overlooking the river. They were to be in Mount Pleasant by 9 am. When they left town the fog was still thick; and it wouldn't lift for about 30 miles. Grandpa negotiated their way back onto Interstate 70 and he cautiously headed west to state highway 89. They then took 89 north.

Just outside of Mt. Pleasant, Sean's Dad pulled over and asked Sean if he would allow Granddad to bless him. This was something that your Grandfather had done repeatedly in his heart, but hadn't externalized since Sean was a boy. Sean agreed.

Your Grandfather prayed over Sean in praise of his humility in accepting help, for Sean to be given strength in the coming weeks and months of treatment, and in gratitude to God for the opportunity for Sean to take a different path. A sense of peace came. And Sean seemed gratified, and somewhat relieved.

Your Grandfather Michael came to regret – deeply regret – not having repeatedly blessed and prayed with his son in the subsequent months. God should have been the center of each of their lives and of their relationship, externally as well as internally. He came see this failure as one of the many that contributed to your Dad's premature death. And of those mistakes he attributed to himself, he was most ashamed of this one.

This wilderness experience was quite different than two years earlier. The big difference was Sean's attitude. He was no longer walled off emotionally.

He was open to suggestions and ready to listen to the counselors and therapists.

And he had a chance to greatly enjoy the outdoors.

This time it was not the tedious or repetitive outdoor activities of simply moving from camp to camp, as it was two years earlier. The activities in this program were more varied in type, and involved the potential for use of more physical skills. There was more adventure: skiing, climbing, and exploring, for example.

Fortunately, Mariah, they have a lot of pictures taken during those weeks. Hopefully you will be able to see some of the beautiful places he experienced. As well the smiles of satisfaction that came to your Dad.

The therapy of the program was integrated into those activities. Sean received a lot of positive feedback, both in therapy and in his physical abilities. He was once again getting the honest feedback anyone with his issues needed. He was not being protected from the truth by denial, which had resumed 14-16 month earlier when he left the organic farm to resume life with his mother.

At this point he seemed to accept and face the reality of himself, of his problems, of his responsibility for the legal problems, and of his need to change.

His Father believed that all the things Sean had heard and experienced two years earlier, in the first wilderness program, had been "percolating" inside of Sean since then. At Second Nature, two years earlier, Sean had come to see the truth of his problems. He had admitted to himself he was addicted to alcohol and drugs, even if reluctantly and not whole heartedly.

My friend thought the months of sobriety on the organic farm in Washington had led Sean to the false sense that he was ready to handle his problems on his own. When his mother extracted him from the farm, he thought he would able to "handle" his addictions and deal constructively with his life without any additional help.

When that failed completely, with his continued drinking and its consequences, he did not revert to denial, as he had before. He was able to admit his failings and accept at least some degree of responsibility.

Sean was ready to make significant changes.

His therapist at Aspiro was Brad Carpenter.

After flunking out of college six years earlier, Sean had, understandably, concluded he was not likely to make it through college. At least not in the traditional manner. Though he could read at a tenth grade level, his dyslexia made reading and writing a very real challenge. And, although he didn't talk about it, he knew his ability to maintain focus (the ADD) also limited the likelihood of success.

Yet, he grew up with his Dad and his Dad's family emphasizing the importance of education.

Your Granddad Michael was certain Sean experienced frustration and shame around this dilemma. And, rather than an exploring attitude, he had adopted the fatalistic attitude. It is very likely that this internal conflict added to his urge to hide in alcohol and drugs.

Brad Carpenter challenged Sean to reconsider his future.

Brad encouraged Sean to allow himself to dream. If there were no barriers, what would Sean really enjoy doing? Sean began to consider. He liked the outdoors. He liked dealing with animals. He liked cooking. He had enjoyed many aspects of the organic farming.

They brainstormed. Sean thought he might really enjoy working on or leading safaris. Safaris! Wow! Wild!

Sean quickly concluded that wasn't possible.

But Brad, rather than simply accept Sean's excuses and give up the idea, helped Sean to hold onto it. They used the internet to seriously explore his dream. They found there were actually places that offered training as a safari guide!

OK. The seed was planted.

Again Sean's barrier: "No way I could accomplish that." he could be heard to lament.

Still, Brad didn't let Sean give up. He didn't allow Sean to take the "that's-not-my-fate" attitude.

But how could he pursue that? Sean was sure there was no way he would get any help, particularly from his Dad, your Granddad, for something like safari-guide training.

Once again, Brad pushed Sean to think about it.

"What was your Dad paying for you (Sean) to be here (in therapy)?"

"What would it cost to get training as a safari guide?"

Brad continued to encourage Sean to dream and to seriously consider his dreams. And Brad was in touch with Granddad weekly. While he didn't share with Sean's Dad the dreams (he wanted Sean to be able to do that), he knew your Grandfather's overall attitudes toward Sean's potential and future. He knew my friend's support for his son.

Granddad was going to be going to a family conference a few weeks later as part of the Aspiro program. Brad and Sean made plans for Sean to share with his Dad at the conference.

Before the conference, Brad told Grandpa there was something Sean wanted to talk to him about in person. A meeting was planned.

My friend imagined he and Sean were going to talk privately. My friend was surprised when Brad asked if he could attend. Granddad sensed Brad was to be there to support Sean.

When Louella heard of the planned meeting, she wanted to be there as well. Granddad acquiesced, as was his nature. She came, sat, and listened. But it was clear Brad orchestrated this to be Sean's meeting with his Father.

During a long break in the conference the four of them sat down.

Your Grandfather shared that he was anxious to hear what Sean wanted to talk about. Anything that would or could have improved their relationship would have been, as they say, "music to his ears."

Sean was nervous.

Hhmmm.

Why?

Sean hesitated a bit, but with Brad's encouragement Sean finally laid out his dream of being a safari guide. He acknowledged it was a far-fetched idea. He seemed embarrassed to have even spoken the idea out loud. He suggested that he already knew Granddad's response would be negative. He almost blamed Brad for forcing him to share the idea.

Your Grandfather was indeed surprised, but he was also fascinated. He followed the logic and was elated Sean was thinking "outside the box." Sean was involved. Sean was exploring his future. Sean was excited by something POSITIVE. Sean was considering something he COULD DO, rather than all the things he couldn't do. Sean was considering possibilities.

Sean was amazed by his Dad's positive attitude.

When Granddad asked for some more details, Sean had them.

What might it cost? Where could such training be received? How likely was Sean to get a paying job after such training? Where could he work?

Sean had answers.

Yes, it was a bit far-fetched, but it still made sense. Granddad promised to give that idea, and his funding of it, serious consideration. Your Grandfather told Sean how excited he was not just with the dream, but, more importantly, the attitude.

Sean was delighted with his Dad's affirming response.

Sean realized that he could dream.

Sean had made another big change.

Chapter 18 -- THE SPIRIT DOESN'T THRIVE IN AN ATMOSPHERE OF CONFLICT

Your Grandpa was delighted Sean was looking positively toward his future. The last time he had seen this in Sean, for more than fleeting pleasures, was way back in 4th grade!

Sean's spirit was being rekindled. He was inspired.

What had destroyed his spirit so long ago?

My friend pondered this too.

Granddad saw how Sean had grown up with his parents in conflict.

They were not just different people when it came to dyslexia.

Their differences permeated their way of living and put them into ever increasing conflict (eventually and notably in how to deal with Sean's problems).

Indicators of differences were present in the early years, while they were still in Espanola, and Sean was under five years of age. Some examples:

- My friend had a tailor hand-make five neckties. He had taken the time to pick out the material, and, in essence, designed them. They were over-sized and a bit gaudy. But he enjoyed wearing them to work because they were full of colorful designs that would catch the eye of the little children that he cared for in his medical work.

One day he found them missing. He asked Louella, his new wife, if she had moved them. She had. She had thrown them out. She simply explained that she didn't like them. So, she had thrown them out. .

How could she do such a thing without telling him or explaining to him? He was dumbfounded, and hurt.

- For their wedding, family and friends had given them over $800, in cash. The two of them agreed to put the money away and to share later in choosing how to use it, thereby honoring those who had gifted it to them.

Several months later Grandpa found the money was missing. As Louella was the only other person in the world who knew where the money had been hidden, he asked her about it.

Initially she denied any knowledge. When confronted with the obvious fact that no one else could have removed the money, she admitted having taken it.

He asked her why? She stated her sister wanted to borrow money.

Your Grandfather told her he would have been happy to lend money to her sister, particularly as they were now family. Why did she do this unilaterally and deceptively? He asked Louella to return the money as soon as it was repaid, and to be forthright and honest with him in the future about such things.

To this day my friend tells me that money has never been replaced. Over the years, he brought it up with Louella several times, in the name of healing and trust. Still she never replaced the money. Your Granddad came to suspect she never really lent the money to her sister.

- The year they married, your Grandfather decided to remodel the old adobe house that was their home. He would put a 1000 square foot addition on for his new family. Given the financial constraints he was under however, your Granddad had to act as de facto general contractor. In managing the construction, it was common of him, as he left to start his 14 hour workday as a doctor, to request that Louella do a 15 minute, 30 minute, or even 2 hour errand or task to keep the work flow going smoothly.

  It was not uncommon for him to come home late and exhausted, ask her about the errand, only to learn that she had failed to carry it out.

  This became a pattern. His frustration deepened into exasperation. One day he found himself sitting on a chair in the tiny laundry room by the back door crying. He was pleading with her for her understanding and cooperation. He was begging her to help him. Things changed a little bit for the better. But only for a few weeks.

- Given his long hours at work your Grandfather left the care of Sean to his wife. But sometimes, at night, when Sean would cry, Granddad would ask Louella to pick

117

up Sean and console him.   More than once she would say "Let him cry. It is good for his lungs."

Grandpa later realized this had not been a few isolated occurrences. Rather, this response indicated an attitude and a pattern Louella had learned from others. And he came to hear from others this had gone on, not just at night but also, during the long hours he was away at work.

Early childhood development studies, he later learned, came to document the negative impact of such parenting.

Fortunately, several years later, by the time Sean's sister was born, Grandpa was present in the house much more of the time. He would go pick her up when she cried. He came to understand his daughter's cries. They were not those of a spoiled child simply wanting to be held. After her need was met, she was content to be put back down.

Sometimes she was ill, as she was prone to ear infections. Her Dad would get up and console her. If he thought she was ill he would diagnose her and would treat her. One night, he remembered very distinctly. She would not stop crying when put down. He stayed up walking with her all night. Louella never got up. He then went to work the next day with no sleep.

He remembered this so vividly because he was so surprised that he did not feel that same fatigue that he usually felt after being up all night in the care of patients (and he had done that many times over the years). He concluded the love and affection for his

118

daughter made the sacrifice and effort very different than the effort that went into care of patients. Energy giving, he would say, rather than energy draining.

A few months after that, Sean's sister went to surgery for her ears.

In those early years Grandpa was so busy that he did not effectively, as head of the household, deal with these issues. Unfortunately, very unhealthy patterns had started. Louella would continue to deceive him when it was convenient for her to do so. She continued to shirk tasks she found difficult, including the discipline-requiring aspects of parenting. Here are some examples.

- When they felt Espanola there was $75,000 of money owed to your Grandfather from work over the past months; accounts receivable, if you will. To collect money he asked Louella if she would mail out the bills rather than pay a collection agency to do so. It was not hard work, only busy work. She agreed.

  However, she never mailed a single envelope. All it would have taken is copying, folding, stamping, and mailing. Nothing mentally or physically challenging.

  It is reasonable to expect that they would have collected at least one third of that money, if only the bills had been mailed.

- They were in Las Vegas for five years. My friend learned after four years that she had been pilfering about $300 a month from a savings account without communicating with him. This was money that was being set aside for a vehicle to replace one of their old

119

ones. When he discovered what had been going on, he found the ongoing deception many times more painful than any money issue. They were not a team.

- Grandpa would ask Louella to help with, or, at least, to appreciate, the financial squeeze they were experiencing. There were mortgages on properties in Espanola (that she wanted him to keep) while the demands of caring for the family were ever-present. Despite repeated requests, she was never willing to collaborate with him in financial planning or budgeting. He felt abandoned and without a partner. Worst, he felt unappreciated and taken for granted, despite all his hard work.

Your Granddad repeatedly tried to help Louella to understand the gravity of her choices and the importance of partnering. He also continually looked within himself to make changes that could help him to be a better husband and father. Here is a list of some of his efforts over the years:

- He took them to a "Medical Marriage" conference in Colorado, so she could be aware of the stresses and challenges marriages experience when one of the spouses is a doctor.
- He encouraged and paid for a Dale Carnegie seminar for Louella.
- A couples retreat through the parish/ Catholic community
- Intentional association and fellowship with highly functioning couples in Las Vegas
- Marriage counseling
- Individual counseling for himself

- Supported and encouraged inspirational books and movies for the family, such as: *Children of a Lesser God, My Left Foot, Lorenzo's Oil,* and *What Love See's*
- A three month leave of absence from employment, in southern California, to work on the marriage and the family
- A request to Louella's parents for help
- More marriage counseling
- A request that the television be turned off to allow for meaningful interaction within the family
- Another request to Louella's parents for understanding and assistance, when they lived in Phoenix, AZ.
- Offer to Louella for her to get education in handling finances
- A personal, forty-day, spiritual retreat for himself to consider options for the relationship
- A legal change in the relationship in an attempt to stop the financial discord/conflict
- A sustained decrease in his work hours to 40-45 hours per week (from ~ 60 hr/week) to spend more time with the family
- A move back to New Mexico to get closer to the support of extended family and friends
- Spiritual counseling, on an individual basis, to look for ways he could change for the sake of the relationship and the family
- Writing a lengthy (close to 100 page) explanation and challenge to Louella hoping to open up dialogue
- Repeated requests to Louella, when she remained in Phoenix after he and the children had moved to New Mexico, for her emotional and temporal support

- Convinced Louella to join him in attending *Retrovaille*, a high-quality, spiritual-based program designed to help couples rebuild a marriage, even after such severe disruption as divorce
- As late as 2011, asked Louella to answer questions in an attempt to open up dialogue

Despite all the efforts, Louella changed little, if at all.

- She had taught Sean to lie to his father.
- She did not honor her husband, and modeled that dishonor to their children.
- Never paid for or offered to help pay for any of the private education of the children.
- Never paid for or offered to help pay for any of Sean's four-plus years of therapy for dyslexia.
- She agreed with Granddad to share in a budget supporting the children, and then fell thousands of dollars behind in her commitment forcing Granddad to pay her share for the children.
- She repeatedly forced Granddad to cover other financial commitments, which she made unilaterally and which she failed to honor.
- She never paid him back, or even tried to pay him back, for his help with her over-spending.
- She never thanked him for helping her with her responsibilities.
- Repeatedly, she got into credit card debt. This included very sizeable amounts owed for penalties as well as interest. As alluded to above, Granddad paid many of these expenses directly or indirectly.
- When she stayed behind in Phoenix to live and Granddad and the two children moved to New Mexico, she began to drink alcohol in a manner she had never done when she lived with Granddad.

- She resumed use of marijuana once she was separated from Granddad
- Later, she allowed marijuana to grow in her home, risking significant legal problems and the loss of her job. She did this despite being aware of the shocking example she was being to a son who was wrestling with alcohol and drug abuse.
- She never apologized for any of the offenses she committed against her husband and her children.
- At the break up she received about $10,000 that had been saved for the children's higher education and she legally committed to using that money for the higher education of the children. She failed to save it for their education.
- She allowed her alcoholic son repeatedly, over many years, to drink in her home, to drink to excess, and to drink with her at social gatherings.
- She helped her alcoholic son get a job at a bar.
- She repeatedly explained away her choices as "no big deal."
- As mentioned, she undermined Granddad's efforts to help Sean. Most notably, but certainly not only, when she tried to keep Sean from attending the first wilderness program and when she pulled him out of the sober living program at Straight Arrow in Washington State.
- She allowed an alcoholic, drug-using girlfriend of Sean's to live with him at her home.
- Later, she invited another emotionally challenged and vulnerable girl, that Sean had had an inappropriate sexual relationship with in an earlier therapeutic program, to move in from out-of-state to live with her and with Sean.
- She committed to learning her role in Sean's alcoholism and making appropriate changes, and

then she failed to honor that commitment. In the months before his death she not only failed to support him in sobriety, she actually drank with him. When confronted with this reality, she exclaimed, "Well, I wasn't going to give up **my drinking!**"

Clearly the conflict between his parents, including their different ways of behaving and treating one another, was at least confusing to Sean. Your Grandfather was convinced these conflict and differences were much, much worse than confusing. That discord was devastating for Sean.

As I mentioned to you before, Mariah, my friend realized that any kid, if given the choices Sean was given, would choose as he had. Louella was extroverted, fun, carefree, and expected little of him. Your Grandfather, on the other hand, was quiet, serious, responsible, and expected much more of Sean. Any child would pick the easier path.

Unfortunately, in following the easier path Sean lost, for years, the opportunities to mature and to develop into a responsible young man. He missed years of maturation that would reasonably be expected to lead to self-confidence and self-discipline. The easier path also led to a lack of integrity, to a lack of internal honesty.

Despite being caught in these parental pincers, Sean was able to develop a positive attitude and self-image while at Aspiro. And he had managed to take the next step in his personal growth.

Chapter 19 -- WHERE TO NEXT?

Sean was ready to move on, and out of the wilderness program. After only 6 weeks!

But where to?

Unlike two years earlier, Sean was willing to consider a program that offered some therapy. But he didn't think he could tolerate a program that had intensive therapy.

Unlike two years earlier, Sean felt he could now deal with some temptation and would not run off to the nearest bar. This opened up possibilities.

Unlike two years earlier, Sean was willing to consider some formal education. The safari-guide dream required some education. But he didn't think he was ready to jump into school full time, and certainly not ready for a four year commitment.

Ms. Cohen's expertise would again be needed.

The possibilities, while expanded, were still limited. Some programs couldn't be considered due to Sean's age, he was already 25 years old. Some couldn't be considered due to Sean's expressed reluctance regarding intense therapy. And some had to be rejected because they involved too much school and formal study.

He would need a program willing and able to accommodate him and to individualize his care. A program willing to adapt to Sean and to dynamically work with him.

That was a tough assignment.

A return to Straight Arrow was seriously considered.

Sean knew Straight Arrow. So, he knew what he would be returning to. Could they set up some therapy for Sean? Ms. Cohen talked with them, and they were willing to try. What about education? There might be some available nearby, but it was not part of their program.

Granddad wanted to know if they would be willing to lower their charges. Sean had proven himself as a very effective laborer when there before. And my friend was still bitter about how they had mishandled Sean's previous departure. Your Granddad wanted a discount, or at least an apology given their screw up in letting Louella take Sean away from the program. When neither was forthcoming, Granddad nixed Straight Arrow as an option.

Some programs were predominately academic. Others were predominately therapeutic.

Finally, a program in Klamath Falls, Oregon, was decided upon. It had some on-site work and claimed that they would help Sean find more definitive, salaried work offsite. They also had on-site therapists. The program offered some structure and it was assumed the monitoring would be adequate and appropriate. There was both a community college and a branch of Oregon Institute of Technology in the town. They were told classes could be arranged.

While not ideal, this program seemed reasonable and they seemed willing to adjust to Sean's unique combination of issues.

Before heading up to Oregon, Sean was allowed to return briefly to Albuquerque.

Technical challenges and logistical issues had to be thought through. How to get Sean to Klamath Falls, Oregon, from Albuquerque, New Mexico? There was no direct or easy route. Should he fly? Multiple stops (and temptations, with risks, including legal risks). Should he go by bus? Or by train? If so, they faced the same issues. Should he go alone? That did not seem prudent. Should someone go with him? If so, who?

Eventually your Grandfather saw that it would be best if he went with Sean. That way Granddad could also meet and talk with those who would be helping Sean. On short notice, he was able to get off work.

It was decided to go by train. It was cheaper, and less convoluted. And, while a longer trip, my friend could spend some needed time with his son.

The trip via Los Angeles took a day and a half. They left Albuquerque in the late afternoon on Monday, March 29, 2011. They arrived in LA early the next morning. A few hours later they pulled out of LA to meander north through California, arriving in Klamath Falls the following morning.

This trip was not so somber or quiet as the trip to Aspiro and Mount Pleasant, Utah, had been. Sean was more relaxed. Actually, he was more self-confident. He seemed determined to move on with his life. He was buoyed by the praise and experiences at Aspiro.

A rental car was dropped off at the Klamath Falls train station for them. They were hungry, having had mostly snacks for the past two days. They found the main drag -- 6th Street -- and cruised it looking for the right spot. They decided on a place called the Black Bear Diner. They had a great breakfast at a fair price. The meal was good enough that they both agreed that they'd like to return someday.

Then they headed back west to the older part of town where the program's buildings were located. They were headed to High Street, between 9th and 10th.

About one block from there, on the corner of High and 8th, they crossed in front of a church, a Catholic church: Sacred Heart. My friend saw this as a wonderful opportunity for Sean. It would be easy for Sean to get to Mass.

His Father encouraged Sean to make time to go to Sunday Mass each week. And, given the convenient location, he encouraged Sean to try to get to Mass during the week. Sean said he would see if he could.

Granddad noted Sean was not at all negative about church, he wasn't enthusiastic either. A feeling of regret passed through my friend. He had not been as good at sharing the faith as maybe he should have been. He wondered if Sean would have had a lot less difficulty in life if he had grown up seeing a more dynamic and active devotion in his parents. He regretted not being more vocal with Sean about his own Christian beliefs.

But they didn't have time to talk much then as they were expected at the program in just a few minutes.

As they met the principles at the program, Sean was engaged. He was ready to do whatever was asked of him. It looked like most of the others enrolled were younger than him. But he had expected that.

Sean and his Dad were shown around the area. The program had two houses near each other. And there was a large, two-story recreational building. This was on 11th and Pine, about 2-3 blocks away from the houses. The houses were part of a residential area just west of the old part of town.

Granddad was given an appointment to have a deeper discussion with the therapist assigned to Sean. In that conference, he walked the therapist through Sean's history and suggested an attitude that might work best with Sean. Your Grandfather thought this fellow to be a bit young. He undoubtedly had credentials, but my friend sensed he had limited experience.

Sean met his roommate. They brought his things in from the car. At least he wasn't going to be sleeping outside as he had the previous seven weeks. However, in reality, Sean didn't seem to mind much being outdoors 24 hours per day.

With Sean settled in, your Grandfather headed back. He had to drive over a low mountain pass to Medford, Oregon. The next morning he would fly out from there.

My friend had to hope his son would continue to grow. Sean certainly had enthusiasm that was not to be found within him two years earlier. But, there had been so much negative behavior and so many poor choices by Sean for so many years that his Father was afraid to be over confident.

Chapter 20 -- CONTINUED PERSONAL GROWTH

At that program, in the coming weeks, Sean would have to address each of the following areas, if he was to successfully turn his life around.

Behavior
> Therapy (Mental Health)
>> Sobriety and abstinence
>>> Spiritual Life
>>>> Work
>>>>> Education

Behavior:
The program in Klamath Falls had structure and expectations.   Participants were divided into three groups. Advancement from one level or group to the next was based on behavior.   There was tighter monitoring and greater supervision, with less liberty, at the first level than at the higher levels.

Based on Sean's accomplishments at Aspiro, and his history of eight months in previous programs, the argument was made for Sean to start at level 2. The program director preferred he start at level one and prove himself first. Sean was assured if he met the criteria to advance he would be allowed to do so.

Sean was determined to progress rapidly. Being on level one was humbling for him. He was a few years older than virtually all of the others at the program and he had "put in his time" in the earlier programs. And, in some ways, he was further along than some of the others.

Therapy:
Sean was assigned to a therapist. The idea of therapy in general, and the therapist assigned to him in particular, were not to his liking. But he was not going to make a big issue of these. He had come to accept he had a problem and he wanted to find a way to overcome it. He kept his commitment to attend sessions and to try to get something out of them.

He didn't get much from the alcohol counselor. She basically followed the Alcoholics Anonymous approach. He tried working through some programmed texts on addiction and alcohol. He seemed to know that he needed to get inside his own mind if he was going to master the demon of addiction.

Your Grandfather thought Sean had come to believe Brad Carpenter, his therapist at Aspiro. Brad had validated Sean's experience with the Alcoholics Anonymous approach. He agreed it didn't work for everyone. Sean knew it hadn't worked for him. Through Brad, Sean came to realize he was not weird or abnormal because AA hadn't helped him improve. And he had tried AA repeatedly, off and on, for over the 10 years[1].

Brad had planted the notion in Sean that there were other approaches. And he had encouraged Sean to explore them with his next therapist. Unfortunately, neither the therapist

---

[1] From junior year high school at 15 years of age until he was 25 years old.

nor the alcoholism counselor at the program offered a different approach.

Despite this, Sean didn't give up. One day he came across a book he thought would help him with the addiction problem. This was surprising because Sean had avoided books.

In one of the phone conversations with his Father, Sean described the book. It was a book on CEBT: Cognitive Emotive (or Emotional) Behavioral Therapy.

As a family physician, your Granddad knew about the ideas behind CEBT. My friend was intrigued that Sean had, on his own, found such book. Sean said how he had read the first chapters which described the therapeutic approach. He wanted someone to walk him through the process. Seeing this resourcefulness from Sean was heartening to his Father.

Moreover, Grandpa knew if Sean learned the CEBT process then he would develop a strong internal (psychological) framework to help him understand and deal with his addiction. And the process, an internal tool, could also help Sean in other aspects of his life as well.

Sean was showing insight and taking initiative.

****

Before we go on, Mariah, you should understand more about CEBT.

C stands for Cognitive. And cognitive refers to thinking. Emotive refers to emotions or feelings. Behavioral refers to action, or what one does. This therapy teaches the learner the relationship between thoughts, emotions, and actions. Once the learner understands that relationship, then he or she is empowered to make choices.

Psychologists learned that people don't just do things (or take actions) for no reason at all. We humans act because of our feelings. We feel pain, we move away. We feel hungry, we look for food. We feel good about someone, we move toward them. We dislike someone, we avoid them. We tend to do what makes us feel good: physically or emotionally. We try to avoid what make us feel bad: physically or emotionally.

Psychologists also learned something that is not always so obvious. They learned that our emotions come from our thoughts.

The reason this is not always so obvious is because often our thoughts are not conscious.

This therapy teaches the student/ learner to become aware of the (often unconscious) thoughts that precede emotions.

Anyone can learn to become aware of preceding thoughts if they practice doing so.

And, with practice and experience, the learner begins to see patterns. The learner begins to see more clearly which emotions lead him or her to act in such a way. And, they learn what thoughts tend to precede which emotions.

Once the student sees the patterns, he/she becomes empowered. She might come to realize many of her behaviors actually originate in thoughts that are untrue or from thoughts that are only assumptions.

The goal, of course, is to master the therapy and thereby become aware of the thoughts that lead to negative behaviors. Once aware of such thoughts, she is now free to consider the thoughts more closely and consciously, rather than simply (usually unconsciously) responding. If the now conscious thought is untrue or only an assumption about what may (or may not be) true, she may well choose a different action or behavior than she would without such awareness.

Can you see how this empowers the learner? She is not under the control of (unconscious) thoughts and assumptions. Rather, she is in control of herself: her thoughts, her emotions, and her behaviors. She has a choice of responses instead of a limited reaction.

****

Unfortunately, no one at the program would actively help Sean with CEBT. They allowed him to read the book. But they didn't help him to learn what was in the book. Nor would they give him any credit for, or even critique, his progress. Sean's Dad was very disappointed with this.

Sobriety and Abstinence:
Unlike two years earlier, he seemed to be OK with the temptations. Despite drinking establishments and alcohol sales just a few blocks down the street; he no longer found the temptation of alcohol or drugs so uncontrollable.

Though no one else but Sean knows with certainty, my friend thought your Dad was sober his entire time there.

Surely he had stress and he had cravings.   But, unlike in the past, he now seemed to have a positive self-image that gave him interior strength to better resist the urges and to go forward.   And, importantly, he had no one tempting him and everyone supporting him in sobriety.

Spiritual Life:
Sean maybe ended up going to Mass once or twice. As your Granddad thought back over these things, after Sean's death, my friend became more and more convinced this was the area where he failed his son the most.

Your Grandfather had a long history of spiritual education. He had gone to Catholic schools for grade school, high school, and college.   More importantly, your Granddad had learned some ways of personal praying that sustained him, at least enough to get through difficult times in life.

The spiritual tradition that he grew up with had surrounded him. It had oozed into him from all sides.   In his experience one's spiritual life was not often verbally discussed or overtly acted upon. It was taken for granted. God, prayer, and religion were simply understood to be a core in life.

Your Granddad now regrets not having shared much more deeply with his son. My friend came to believe that he should have shared the how and the why of a personal relationship with God. He came to believe doing so might have made all the difference in Sean's life.

In defense of your Grandfather, however, I know he would urge and remind Sean, with virtually every phone call, to go to Mass and to pray. Sean would agree. But there was a sense Sean was only agreeing to avoid any confrontation. And your Grandfather did not follow up on his words, to see if they had been acted upon. Now, his son is gone, and can't tell him what was really going on in his heart.

This is a source of great pain for your Grandfather.

Work:
Part of Sean's agreement was that he would be engaged in productive activity. The preferred activities agreed upon were to be money-generating employment and/or education.

Initially, the program kept him active on a number of their interior action projects. One that caught Sean's fancy, even as the program was being considered, was an organic garden. As you know he loved being outdoors. And he felt very good about the experience he had gained during those many months in Washington State.

The program had access to an acre, several miles south of the town. In addition, they had a small greenhouse behind the house he shared with others.

He would go out to the one acre site whenever he could. It was fenced in, as there were wildlife nearby that would have been happy to feast on any young plants. The watering/irrigation system needed repair and modification. Sean was by his nature interested and adept at fixing such things. Sean's primary or preferred "learning type" had been determined, years earlier, to be visual-spacial . He could readily see how things are -- or should be -- organized in space.

Sean was an active and eager participant as they chose which plants to grow, as they laid out the garden rows, and as they planted.

Another project he helped with was the building of a sound-proof room in the large recreation building a couple of blocks from their housing. That room would allow those who were musically inclined to have a place to practice without disrupting the rest of the building.

Sean really had many talents that had lain dormant while he wandered aimlessly for so many years due to the lack of self-confidence and lack of self-discipline. It was great for his Dad to know that Sean was experiencing the positive feedback we all thrive on in life.

However, when it came to finding a paying job, Sean bumped up against barrier after barrier. He picked up a few odd jobs through people at the program. But nothing consistent or meaningful. No regular or full-time employment.

Sean explained the barriers to his Dad. First, Klamath Falls was a small town and the businesses were physically spread out. And the public transportation was very limited. Sean said he could not get a clear, consistent commitment from program personnel for transportation. This transportation barrier made looking for a job limited, and committing to a job questionable.

The second barrier was communication. At level one, he was not allowed to have his cell phone. So any calls to or from prospective employers had to go through the program director. And the director's schedule and variable location made it difficult for Sean to be in contact with prospective employers.

Third, as in many small towns, jobs were filled by "who you know." Sean pointed out that employers would, logically, have a hiring preference for someone they knew. Or for someone who was referred by someone they knew and trusted. Why would they pick a young man from out of the area and who had a history of alcohol or drug problems?

Your Granddad wanted to believe that Sean, despite his past manipulation and lying, was being honest. My friend didn't believe his son was lying to him, as he had so often before. But he couldn't be absolutely certain. They did not have a long relationship of trust.

Clearly, something was different however. His Dad noticed Sean was communicating with more thoughtfulness. Sean was explaining and even defending himself better verbally. In the past, such interaction would have been characterized by his agitation and frustration. And he wouldn't have persisted in order to make a point or explain a thought as he was now doing. Your Grandfather had been aware that Sean's previous patterns were due, at least in part, to his ADD. Sean was finding a way around barriers, internal and external.

Despite obstacles, Sean was continuing to make progress on a number of fronts.

Education:
As he arrived in late March, the timing was out of sync with the academic year. His interest in trying to go back to school, however, was a marked change from his previous resistant (and fatalistic) attitude toward school and toward

education. That attitude had taken him nowhere for most of six years.

As part of the agreement in choosing the Klamath Falls program, it was agreed that Sean could attend classes while there. As mentioned, the town had a community college as well as the main campus of Oregon Institute of Technology (OIT). His Dad had agreed to help Sean financially with school, if he would put forth genuine measureable effort.

Sean took initiative. He looked at options. Understandably and appropriately, he didn't think he was ready to start a full college program as offered at OIT. Besides, as a student from out of state it would have been much more expensive. But he was genuinely interested in trying school once again. He must have come to realize his future, without some solid education beyond high school, was limited.

However, he still was afraid. He was probably afraid of failing again. He wanted to go slowly with only a couple of classes initially.

He acquired a catalog for the local community college. He sought out details such as location and dates for the summer session. He considered courses. He talked with his Dad about options.

Behavior:
Unfortunately, all was not perfect in this area. Sean had allowed himself to get involved, sexually, with a girl who was also enrolled in the program.

By the program's rules and structure, he wasn't supposed to have more than passing verbal contact with the girls. They were housed separately.

When his relationship, and the nature thereof, was discovered, much negativity set in. The program (that is, the people running or working at the program) didn't see this as a learning opportunity (for the young people involved or for themselves). They took an attitude that seemed vindictive. It seemed to your Granddad that, as a result of this inappropriate behavior, others made Sean out to be a "problem" rather than a person with a problem.

But you know, Mariah, when he was first told of Sean's inappropriate sexual activity, my friend found that he, too, took the wrong attitude. He found himself upset with Sean and very disappointed. He was frustrated. He was even tempted to give up on Sean when he learned of the foolish and selfish decision Sean had made.

It was the educational consultant, Cynthia Cohen, who helped your Grandfather to see Sean's mistake differently. Her reasoning made sense. She suggested Sean's mistake was a sign that he lacked maturity. She also pointed out the program itself bore a portion of responsibility. Their monitoring had been too lax.

This blunder undoubtedly played a role in keeping Sean from advancing to the next level.

However, the program refused to renegotiate what was now to be expected of him in order to advance to the next level. And Sean began to feel trapped. Once again, he felt punished rather than encouraged. He did not know what was being asked of him in order to proceed.

Paradoxically, this challenge of Sean being trapped at level one helped to bring Sean and his father closer together. He and his Dad had begun, for the first time in years, talking to each other. Among other things, Sean shared his frustration with the program's refusal to advance him. Sean was actually describing his feelings. These insights, and the ability and willingness to share on an emotional level, were things that would have been impossible for him only two years earlier.

His Dad agreed to look into the program's refusal to advance him. And he agreed to support Sean's position if the program failed to give an objective reason for holding him back. But, at the same time, your Granddad did what came naturally to him. He urged Sean to take the "can-do" attitude described in Chapter 13. He recommended that Sean focus on the things he could do, even while he couldn't influence what seemed to be some unfair treatment..

He could concentrate on the therapy, on getting work, and on looking into his education.

And Sean agreed.

The Visit:
It was about this time, in late May, that your Grandfather and Sean's sister, Maria-Teresa, went up to Oregon to see Sean.

Back in February, your Granddad had come to realize he could now be more involved in Sean's life. And by late May it would be months since Sean had seen his sister. She would have the time for a trip then. It would be after her spring semester ended and before she would start her summer work.

The timing would also allow my friend to support Sean as best he could.

As I said, he had some uncertainties about Sean's truthfulness with all that was happening up there. Over the years, Sean had become a master at manipulating his good-hearted father. While your Granddad very much wanted to believe all Sean was telling him, he wanted to know with more certainty the truth of what was actually happening. Going to Klamath Falls would give him a chance to see firsthand.

They too went up by train. The same path Sean and his Dad had taken two months earlier.

It turned out to be a fun trip. There are a number of pictures from the trip that your Grandfather treasures.[2] Hopefully, you will get to see them.

During the visit, the three of them visited Lava Beds National Monument in northern California, not too far south of Klamath Falls. And they drove all the way up to Crater Lake. It is a beautiful, high-elevation lake that was still a winter wonderland in late May. They bowled. And they all relaxed and enjoyed each other's company.

They visited the one-acre garden of the program. Sean proudly showed them the sound-proof room at the recreation center he had spent so much time on. Granddad

---

[2] You may have seen these. Maria-Teresa had the pictures framed and she gifted them to her Dad a few months after the trip.

justly praised him for the quality of his workmanship despite the lack of any formal construction training. It was obvious that Sean's visual-spacial learning type took naturally to that kind of work.

And, as expected, your Grandfather talked with directors, counselors, and housemates.

He concluded that Sean was telling the truth. And, except for his foolish interaction with the girl, Sean seemed to be trying hard to keep his commitments. Unfortunately, your Granddad couldn't get the program to commit in a number of areas where Sean needed support.

A part of the problem was that the program was in the midst of its own turmoil. As a result of poor judgment, they had to dismiss one of the therapists. And it was Sean's therapist. Sean was not the only one affected. There were a number of others. The instability rippled throughout the program.

My friend found himself, once again, encouraging Sean to focus on what he could do. And he encouraged Sean to accept what he could not do.

He could apologize for his behavioral mistake and not repeat it.

He could hope for a better relationship with his new therapist and continue to read the CEBT book.

He could back off on the fruitless efforts at finding a paying job and put more effort into educational possibilities

After the Visit: Sean did all of those.

Behavior:
He made it clear to the program personnel he was aware
that he had made a big mistake in the sexual relationship.
And he made every effort to demonstrate clearly to
everyone at the program he was not ever alone with any
girl anymore. He did this for the remainder of his time
there.

Therapy:
Unfortunately, when it came to therapy, the new therapist
was overwhelmed. Sean claimed to like her, as a person.
But their schedules conflicted and they never met regularly.
Your Grandfather certainly didn't hear much from her.
Therapy smoldered.

Education:
Sean turned his energy toward the educational front.

As he considered his options he came up with the idea of
taking a class they offered at the community college on
drug use and addiction.

Granddad was both surprised and skeptical that Sean
wanted to learn other aspects of drugs and alcohol. He
worried Sean had multiple reasons for his interest.
Granddad remembered the first wilderness program,
Second Nature, had essentially guaranteed Sean a job if he
maintained sobriety and prepared himself to be a counselor.
Such a class might have helped employment options

someday.   However, he also feared if Sean ever resumed drug use the new knowledge could be misused.

The course description follows:

An examination of commonly abused drugs with emphasis on the physical, psychological, and behavioral consequences of these drugs. Includes drug chemistry, physiological effects of drug use upon the body, and specific treatment formats and techniques.

With mixed feelings his Dad agreed.

The second course he decided upon was college algebra. Sean had gone to a good high school. And even though he had not applied himself, he had been exposed to algebra. Indeed, somehow he had completed good college preparatory math classes.

He signed up for the classes. The summer session started in June.

The community college he attended was on the east edge of town, about six miles from his program. Transportation had to be arranged. However, if necessary, he knew he was in good enough condition to walk, or even jog, back to his quarters.

Unfortunately, that happened. One day his program-designated ride forgot about Sean. And after waiting for hours, he decided to walk back. He safely returned with no drinking or any other misconduct. Nonetheless, he found himself accused of wrong doing, for not continuing to wait for his ride. He knew the accusation was unjust.

But he did not fly off the handle or become defensive as he might have in the past.

It became clear there needed to be significant changes if Sean was to prosper at this program.   Before leaving from Aspiro, the program had promised to individualize care for Sean. Clearly that was not happening.

The question was: would it happen or could it happen?

Chapter 21 -- A POOR MATCH ENDS

The program sponsored a family conference to be held the last weekend in June. June 25th to the 27th, 2010.

The month between his May visit to Sean and the family conference was very frustrating for your Grandfather.

As mentioned, there seemed to be more obstacles than opportunities for Sean. Sean was increasingly discouraged and the positive enthusiasm with which he entered the program was waning.

Another concern of his was that Louella was not actively involved in making the changes she had promised. Unlike the Aspiro program, it seemed to him that this program was not actively engaging Louella. He knew, from his experience with her over the previous decade, that she was unlikely to take initiative in learning about her role as Sean's enabler.

Adding to his dissatisfaction, it seemed he was managing more of Sean's care and therapy than the program was.

Nonetheless, he continued to be encouraging to Sean, despite his own frustrations.

There had to be a change. Either the program had to make accommodations for Sean and actively engage Louella, or... ? Or what? He was not aware of a good alternative.

If this program failed, or if Sean failed, then it was back to the detention center, back to New Mexico, and back to the environment that facilitated Sean's downward spiral.

My friend headed to the June family conference with plans to get a pledge from the program to stick by their commitment. He wanted them to commit to:

- Transportation support for Sean
- Stop the vindictiveness
- Give Sean therapy, particularly the CEBT
- Facilitate his education
- Actively involve Louella in her change, taking the initiative which she was not likely to do
- Give Sean a concrete set of expectations he was to meet in order to earn advancement to the next level

Your Grandfather was tense as the weekend came. He flew with Louella to Reno, via Salt Lake City. They drove a rental car from there to Klamath Falls.

Along the way, he tried to explain things. She appreciated the external barriers and challenges Sean faced. But, once again, she played down, minimized, or failed to appreciate the crucially important psychological issues that both she and Sean faced.

But it was fun to see Sean. And he was very happy to see them.

The weekend program itself was pleasant enough. But it did not go into the depth needed. It did not teach parents to fully appreciate their role in the problems their young children were facing. The parents were not challenged to change.

During a break on Saturday, Sean's Dad was able to talk with a program director. He shared his frustrations. The director seemed to hear your Granddad. But he offered no changes.

Curiously, that evening, the director publicly expressed his delight in the conversation he had had with your Granddad. It was then that he realized the director had missed the essence of my friend's communication. He had asked the director what changes were to be made, he wasn't just talking to vent or simply feel heard.

Later that evening or early the next morning, your Grandfather demanded that a conference be held before he and Louella left town. He asked that all the pertinent individuals involved be present at the same time. He desperately wanted to avoid the triangulation[3] that had played a major role in Sean's difficulties at the program – and throughout his life.

----

[3] Triangulation is when a person, instead of going directly to another with whom they have an issue or a problem, goes instead to a third party. This creates the triangle. The two with the issue do not directly address their problem. This seldom solves any problem and usually complicates things because the third party does not and cannot accurately or fairly represent either of the other two parties.
When confronted with a problem, Louella consistently refused to directly address the issue. Thus, the problem or issue would remain unresolved. Sean grew up with this dysfunction and was often caught in the middle of the triangle.
His therapist at the next program, at Clean Adventures, would recognize this. He tried to teach Sean to recognize and stay out of such triangulation.

Who was to be there?

- Sean
- His Dad
- Louella
- The program directors – both husband and wife
- Sean's assigned therapist
- The psychiatrist (who actually had little if any contact with Sean)
- Sean's counselor and/or the alcoholism counselor

The meeting was arranged. And they all met an hour or so after the formal conference ended on Sunday.

The meeting was tense.

Sean was tense. He knew everyone was present because of him.

His Father did everything he could, before and at the beginning of the meeting, to make it perfectly clear to Sean this meeting was not because Sean was a problem. Rather, the meeting was needed because the others present had not clearly agreed upon how to help Sean with his problems. Your Granddad knew this distinction was CRUCIAL to Sean's attitude. Sean had only recently begun to experience himself as a person with problems rather than a person who was a problem.

As his Dad had asked for the meeting, he also requested he be allowed to lay out the issues from his point of view. He stated clearly, as he began, that he was prepared to listen to and to consider the point of view each and every other person present.

Unfortunately, as he expressed his position, he was interrupted by others who were not willing to let him finish. In particular, the director (husband) started defending himself and his program from what he perceived as your Granddad's attack, rather than your Granddad's frustration.

The therapist, who had not had any substantial contact with Sean in the previous four weeks, also began to defend herself. Both claimed Sean was the problem.

Your Grandfather had repeatedly quizzed Sean prior to the meeting to probe and to determine if Sean had been obstructing his own care. He was convinced Sean had consistently acted reasonably. So your Grandfather asked Sean to defend himself and to share his perceptions. Astonishingly, those from the program were not ready to allow a program enrollee to speak up in this manner. When he did so they twisted things so as to blame him rather than accept ANY responsibility for the failures.

My friend saw things now from a different light. Nonetheless, he still felt squeezed from many sides.

The program, on one side, was not working with him to acknowledge and address the real needs of Sean.

On another side, there was Louella, who had for years manipulated him, lied to him, and undermined him, even when it came to his help for Sean. At this meeting, she was not asking for or even acknowledging her need for help. Despite her commitment in February, she was unable to describe any significant change. This was one of the key issues for Sean's long term health and Sean's Dad pushed to have it addressed.

On a third side, Sean had only recently begun to build an honest relationship with Grandpa. And that was virtually all by telephone.

On a fourth side, Granddad did not have an alternative. If he pulled his financial support from this program, then he would be removing Sean from the program. But where would Sean go next? Back to jail was a distinct possibility.

Everyone at the meeting had at least something to gain by Sean's continuing at the program. Everyone, that is, except your Grandfather.

The directors and the employees of the program would get paid.

Louella would not be challenged to change (by this program), and she would not have to witness her son going to jail.

Sean, by staying in the program, would avoid jail and the consequences of the charges against him.

My friend felt so alone and unsupported. And by the very people he thought should or would be helpful.

He actually begged at the meeting for someone at the table to help him.

None would.

The other program director (the wife) expressed feelings for my friend and his frustration. But she offered nothing concrete from the program, saying only that it was hard to help Granddad.

The program director (the husband) kept his defensive position. Indeed, he was furious your Grandfather had held the therapist – or the program -- accountable for her failures to work with Sean.

The therapist herself offered to work with Sean, but then listed reasons why that would be difficult. She was not accommodating. She did not agree to even consider the CEBT. And she did not agree to actively work with Louella.

Louella, for her part, was not about to acknowledge herself as an obstacle to Sean's progress. She did not claim to want or to need any special attention from the therapist. This made my friend look like he was asking for something unusual from the program.

Interestingly, of all present, Sean, while conflicted, seemed to understand his father's position the best.

For his part, however, Sean was conflicted.

He must have been desperately afraid. In some way his future was being determined

But he also knew he had changed. He knew he had been trying. He knew he had made a big mistake with the girl, but he also knew he had confessed. And he knew he had made all the changes he could make to assure everyone he would not repeat that mistake. He had consistently done all else asked of him. It was clear he was willing to continue his path of change.

Your Grandfather was torn.

The meeting demonstrated this program was not a match for Sean. His Father concluded he had to pull Sean out.

But he had no plan on how to proceed from there. He knew such a plan would have to be developed. And he thought they had only two, or maybe three, days to do so. If Sean was not under supervised care, then he would have to be taken back to Albuquerque and to the control of the judges there.

Of all the issues facing my friend, the one that troubled him the most was Louella's persistent failure to accept, acknowledge, and deal with her own role in Sean's problems. She had made but little change since her commitment in February. And, it was now the end of June.

On the surface, she was very willing to help look for an alternative program for Sean. She saw the need for that change. But she was not about to acknowledge her need for change.[4]

However, on that afternoon, at the end of the family conference in June of 2010, my friend had to focus primarily on Sean. He asked himself: would there be

---

[4] It seemed to me, Mariah, that your Grandpa came to a realization, even as he was relating these things to me (and that was not long after your Dad's death). He came to see, too late, that Louella must have been walled off emotionally. She was probably walled off emotionally in the same way Sean had been walled off before he went to the first wilderness program, at Second Nature. He wondered if it would ever be possible to break through her (psychological) defenses.

155

another program and another chance for Sean? Or would
Sean have to be sent back?

Chapter 22 -- WHERE TO NEXT, AGAIN

After the meeting, Sean, his Dad, and Louella went to talk. It was a very pretty day and only mid-afternoon. They settled on a picnic table at the Veteran's Memorial Park, on Main Street, near the river and the lake, a few blocks from their motel.

They reviewed what had happened. They talked about what was said -- and what was not said -- at the meeting. And they reconsidered, each from their own point of view, what had happened and what had not happened over the past few hours and the past four months. Sean expressed his appreciation to his Father. He had felt his Dad's support as he defended himself at the meeting. That was clearly a plus for their relationship.

All three agreed it made no sense for Sean to stay with this program, not under the circumstances.

But what was the alternative? They started throwing out ideas, hoping to regain the momentum Sean had had when he started the Klamath Falls program.

- There was a school up in Bend, Oregon, Sean had heard about. What about school up there if a program could be found?
- Some of Sean's contacts from Aspiro were in different programs. What about one of them?
- What about a couple of programs in Utah that had been considered while he was still at Aspiro?

As they talked, a phone call came in to your Granddad. It was Cynthia Cohen, the educational consultant. "Wow!" he thought, "Was this coincidental or had she already heard about the meeting?" As he picked up the call my friend wondered if she was going to stick up for the program and urge that Sean stay. He walked a short distance from Louella and Sean so he could hear her better and so that the other two could talk.

Ms. Cohen had heard what happened. To my friend's surprise she thought it might be a good thing for Sean to change programs.

Your Grandfather hadn't appreciated how closely Ms. Cohen had stayed involved with Sean's progress. She reminded him she had been uncertain about this program from the start. It was obvious she was aware of much that had happened and much that had not happened over the past four months. While disappointed, she was not entirely surprised by the events.

Most importantly, she was optimistic another program could be found. She was encouraging.

This phone call and her support was a big boost for my friend. Before her call he was still wondering if he had done the right thing to put pressure on the program, urging it to accommodate Sean's needs. He wondered if he had, by pushing, actually put Sean at risk. She assured him he hadn't. She said she would do all she could to help.

Her support was enough to propel them forward. Your Grandfather's "can-do" attitude kicked in, with Sean joining in. The search for the next step, the flurry of activity, had started.

They soon were back at the motel, just blocks away, using the internet, to gather information. Cynthia Cohen suggested programs for them to look into and promised to get back to them.

In the midst of this, the decision to pull Sean from Klamath Falls was formally carried out in a conversation between your Grandfather and the program director. It was agreed Sean would spend the evening with his parents and return to the program that night for sleep. It was not yet clear how long it would take to transition.

Coincidentally, there had been previous arrangements for Sean to leave for New Mexico in just a few days for a Fourth of July visit to New Mexico. It was possible however, that if the airline could accommodate them, Sean might be able to return with his Father and Louella on their return trip to Albuquerque the next day.

By the end of the evening they had learned that if Sean was willing to go "standby" then there was a good chance he would make it to Albuquerque the next day. It was even possible he would end up on the same flights as his parents. They decided to take the risk and to give that plan a try.

Even as those flight arrangements were being made, websites of various programs were viewed and reviewed. Fortunately, my friend had brought a laptop computer and fortunately they had booked a motel room with Internet access.

Sean and his Father were in agreement regarding therapy at the next program. They both wanted a program that would use, or, at least, support the CEBT approach.

And on the educational side, Sean expressed a willingness to consider a more aggressive educational plan, as long as it would accommodate his dyslexia and ADD. It seemed the few weeks of classes Sean had just completed had made him more confident in his abilities.

They looked at and discussed a number of websites and programs suggested by Ms. Cohen.

The marathon efforts were broken only by a pleasant Oriental dinner half a block down the street.

It wasn't long before 10 pm arrived, and Sean was due back at the program.

His Father counseled Sean to go back with a positive attitude. It would do no good for Sean to criticize the program or anyone there. No good would come from that. People, including Sean and his Dad, may have negative feelings, but to disparage others was not going to accomplish anything positive for anyone.

Sean accepted the advice and agreed to follow it. My friend thought: This is the same young man who had for over eight years, until less than six months earlier, refused virtually all advice from his Father. Your Granddad saw Sean was continuing to mature.

Sean's departure from the program the next morning was cordial. By that time, it seemed, everyone involved had concluded it was best for Sean and the program to separate.

The six hour drive to Reno from Klamath Falls was spent thinking and sharing. Information from and about different programs continued to be discussed. The atmosphere was a mixture of hope and angst.

Granddad and Louella dropped Sean off at the airport for a possible earlier stand-by flight to Salt Lake City. The two of them went for a bite to eat, and then dropped off the rental car. When they later arrived at their gate, Sean was still there.

With so much on everyone's mind the discussion of options quickly resumed. As they waited for the flight they once again went online and searched or reviewed various programs and options via the Internet. Some phone calls were made and discussions with possible programs began.

His Father had always believed Sean could and should get a college education. He knew there had to be schools in the US that could and would accommodate students with the same limitations as Sean's. The challenge was to find one where a monitored therapeutic program was also available to help with the alcohol/drug problem.

Your Granddad kept thinking about a school in Arizona, Prescott College. He had heard about it from different sources over many years. Your Grandfather had worked in Prescott for about six months, years earlier, when they lived in Phoenix. He had heard a little bit about Prescott College then. One of the directors of the Klamath Falls program, the wife, had graduated from Prescott College. She had shared a little bit about the school with him when he and Maria-Teresa visited.

Sean's Dad went to the Prescott College website and found it very interesting. The following is from the Prescott College webpage that lays out the academic model used.

> The College ensures that students are given multiple and frequent opportunities to learn in authentic situations – through seminar-style classes that promote participation and dialogue, practicum and internship experiences, independent studies, and field experiences. A Prescott College education is based on the idea that students are in control of their learning, and learn best through self-direction, experiential learning, and real-life experience.
>
> This approach to education is both engaging and academically rigorous. Students are expected to assume an active role as they travel, mesh with local communities, conduct field studies, participate in faculty research, and apply their knowledge to real-life problems. Faculty members are guides and coaches who help the students acquire this knowledge. Prescott College is not simply an alternative. It is an entirely different way to help support learners in their search for knowledge.

My friend was intrigued.

He brought the idea of Prescott College to Sean. Initially Sean was hesitant. He was reluctant to seriously consider, much less commit to, a four year school or program of study. The discussion, however, was not all at once. The Prescott College idea came up here and there over several days.

If Prescott could be worked out, a plus would be its location. Presumably, Prescott would be far enough from New Mexico for Sean to be away from past temptations. Yet it would be close enough for some contact with family.

Sean went to the website. The possibility percolated. If the school was to be a possibility then a treatment program in Prescott was mandatory. Without such a therapeutic program, the school was not an option.

Eventually, my friend decided to call Prescott College. He spoke with someone in the admissions department. He was very open and straight-forward about Sean's academic challenges – the dyslexia and the ADD – as well as Sean's present circumstances with addiction, therapy, and the law. The admissions advisor listened attentively, seemingly unfazed.

She thought the school could be ideal for Sean. Most of the classes were outside. Teaching was experiential and action-oriented. There was not a great deal of classroom work nor was there a great deal of reading. This reinforced what had been explained in the "academic model" described above.

She shared that many of the students had challenges that made a traditional college experience difficult, or even impossible, for them. If that were so, my friend thought, Sean might feel at home there. Not so different, or out of place.

She also said they had a number of students who wrestled with alcohol problems. She added there were active plans for special accommodations for such students.

He asked if she knew anything about therapeutic programs in Prescott. No, but she thought she could put him in touch with others at or affiliated with the school who did know about such possibilities.

Sean's Dad got off the phone enthused. He calmed himself a little bit, not wanting his hopes to get too high. Then he shared with Sean what the admissions counselor had told him. Sean, too, found the comments heartening.

They decided to dig in deeper.

They considered academics. What about a "major"-- or primary area of study? Sean was not interested in committing to a "major" but he was very interested in a number of the classes the school offered.

Sean was pleased and surprised there we classes involving organic farming. He seemed interested in classes on environmental issues. And, he was curious about some of the classes in adventure education.

It was time to seriously search options for therapy in Prescott. Through the Internet they got some leads. The Prescott College admissions counselor came through with some contacts. And Ms. Cohen helped look into Prescott programs as well.

One website caught Granddad's eye. That site mentioned that cognitive-behavioral therapy was part of their approach to treatment. He called. He spoke to the director, and later to the therapist. It seemed to him this program would support Sean's preference for CEBT.

After discussion with Sean they both found an optimism growing.

Even as other possibilities were considered, a trip to Prescott would make sense.

Chapter 23 -- PRESCOTT IT IS

When to make the trip?

If Sean was to get into another treatment program without having to go back before the judge....

If Sean was to start in a school at the beginning of the next semester, then the sooner a decision was made, the better.

 If Prescott was not going to work out, then they needed time to make arrangements elsewhere.

While all of these things were happening, your Grandfather had to continue to work. When could he get time off to make the trip? They couldn't go on a weekend and expect to find all the people available they needed to talk with.

Arrangements were finalized to leave Albuquerque Thursday, July 15th.   If the trip was successful, then Sean would stay.

If.
> If Sean found the program acceptable.
> If his Dad found the program acceptable.
> If the therapeutic program would accept Sean.
> If an appropriate school plan in Prescott could be arranged.

If Sean was willing to try whatever school plan could be arranged.
If a school plan could be afforded.
If the program would allow Sean to attend the school.

They left Albuquerque with many "ifs."

With a reasonably early start they would arrive in Prescott mid-afternoon.

This trip was more relaxed and comfortable for each of them than had been the two earlier trips they had taken together that year: to Aspiro and to Klamath Falls. They visited. They discussed options. They listened to some music.

As soon as they arrived they headed for the program, as planned.

Sean and his Dad met with Bobby Patton, the director, and Wes Kitchens, the therapist. My friend laid out Sean's history. Sean explained where he was therapeutically. Bobby Patton described the program. And Mr. Kitchens described the therapeutic approach.

They felt Sean was in the right place therapeutically for the program. They offered cognitive-behavior therapy while simultaneously expecting an AA approach. The AA approach was modified however. More insight was shared at AA meetings. And a greater variety of AA meetings were available.

They shared that Prescott actually had a large "recovery" community. There were a number of programs in town and many graduates of the programs had settled down in Prescott. If Sean really wanted to make the change to sobriety, there were opportunities to do so.

And they would be willing to let him go to school while attending the program.

Sean was satisfied. His Father was satisfied.

They headed for the motel, pleased with the good fortune so far.

It was summertime, so the day was still long. They decided to go together for a run in the surrounding mountains. Sean and his Dad had not worked out together since many years earlier, when Sean was in grade school and they were both still playing soccer. This was a treat for my friend, but there was also a wonderful problem for him as well. He had to experience and accept Sean was now in better physical condition than he was. Sean was in good shape physically. He ran farther and faster than his Dad. My friend was proud of his son's growth.

The next day they were up reasonably early and headed off to the Prescott College admissions office. The school's academic approach was reviewed and reiterated. They described a great deal of flexibility and a willingness to allow Sean to explore options even as he took classes.

While cautious still about school and his long-term prospects, Sean seemed to like what he heard.

They then discussed finances. Your Grandfather explained to them, as he had to Sean, that he could not afford to put Sean through a private college. He could guide Sean and give him advice, but financially he had already raided his retirement funds to get Sean the therapeutic help he had needed so desperately. My friend had, by that time, already spent well over $100,000 on the programs since 2008.

The admissions counselor thought Sean could get loans and grants. But the school was expensive. Even with grants, Sean would be taking on considerable debt.

Would he be – realistically -- likely to pay off such a debt when finished? What were the chances Sean would be able to find appropriate, good-paying work when he graduated? Was he willing to take on the debt? And, remember, he had not even paid off the debt he had incurred from his one semester at New Mexico State University years ago.

All of those questions were raised and considered over the day.

A financial counselor found Sean could get the financial aid, despite his preexisting debt. Sean was willing to take the risk. His Father thought Sean could do it. They both thought the school to be a good match for Sean given his challenges. It seemed Sean could and would get just the kind of support he needed at this institution.

They were both pleased. And Sean was up-beat and optimistic once again, as he had been upon leaving Aspiro; yet he was still appropriately apprehensive.

All had gone as well -- even better – than they could have reasonably expected.

My friend touched base with Cynthia Cohen, who had remained involved and supportive. She thought the plan was reasonable, though she was not directly familiar with the therapeutic program.

They decided to "go for it."

They went back to admissions and financial aid. They started the paperwork and made arrangements to get high school transcripts to the college.

Later in the afternoon they went back and shared the decision with Bobby Patton and the program. The program would take him.

They went back to the motel, picked up Sean's things, and checked out early.

They went to the designated program house. They met and greeted the other inhabitants and counselors. They dropped off Sean's things. They said warm "good-byes." And they had a parting hug.

Sean settled in.

And Sean's Dad began his evening ride back to New Mexico.

Lots to think about for six plus hours.

Lots to be thankful to God for.

But, then again, your Granddad came to think he was never grateful enough to God for all those blessings.

Chapter 24 -- FINALLY, A SUSTAINED PERIOD OF GROWTH; AT LEAST FOR SEAN

Many things went as well or better than could have been expected.

Thankfully, the therapeutic program allowed a great deal of flexibility when it came to class work. Given the unique and relatively unorthodox approach of the school, the program's flexibility was a significant piece of good fortune. School required Sean to be away from Prescott for days at a time on projects or outings. This meant he would also be away from the program for days at a time.

The first month of school was to be a test for Sean. He shared with his Dad how he was anxious about the expectations. The month would determine if he could handle the work and the responsibilities of college; and if he could adapt and adjust to this particular education style/school.

A significant part of that orientation month was devoted to writing. To his surprise, Sean found he was able to handle the writing. That was a major hurdle, mostly psychologically, for him. Although he had, through those five years of sacrifice, learned to read and write despite his dyslexia, he had not come to an internal peace and awareness that his abilities would be enough for most college level work. He had harbored a fear of failure.

During that first month, he also came to understand that, fortunately, many of the classes in which he would be involved did not require a great deal of writing, or even a great deal of reading. He came to trust, just as the school had described, much of the learning was experiential or "hands on" learning

Mariah, as I mentioned to you before, your Dad's primary learning style was visual-spacial. His second most preferred learning mode was bodily-kinesthetic. Prescott College was designed to accommodate such learning styles. Most traditional colleges emphasize and use the logical-mathematical or the linguistic learning styles.

The first month of orientation went well academically. It also went well socially. The school was actually quite small in total numbers of students and in class size as well. It was relatively easy to get to know, directly or indirectly, many of the other students. He started some friendships and developed many contacts.

Through those contacts he quickly came to understand how the school functioned. He learned about the various areas of study. His other classes that first semester, in the fall of 2010, were New Student Seminar I: Wilderness & Civilization: Explorations in the New West, New Student Seminar II: Outdoor Education & Recreation, and New Student Seminar III: Writing Workshop.

Sean had settled into the therapeutic program in July and early August, before school started. The program was male only. His Father felt this was crucial to much of Sean's progress over the year. The men treated him fairly and based on his behavior. There was no manipulation or

171

games playing. And, as he did all that was asked and expected of him, he received praise and positive feedback.

Sean did what was asked. Sean responded to the structure others placed around him. He learned to work within the externally applied limitations and boundaries. He showed up when and where he was expected to. He went to AA meetings as expected. He carried out tasks and duties as required or assigned. He was lauded by many for his ability to juggle all that was being expected of him. He kept long and busy days.

The program offered a family conference twice a year. Unfortunately, the fall program conflicted to some extent with Sean's class activities. In addition, Louella chose to opt out, explaining they had just had the family conference in Oregon the summer before. And Sean's sister would have a hard time making the conference given her school responsibilities.

At Christmas 2010, Sean came back to New Mexico for the holidays. Everyone, family and friends, noticed a marked difference in Sean. He was much more open. He was much more communicative. He had positive experiences to share. He was honest and frank about his issues with alcohol and addiction. It was clear he had grown a great deal in 2010.

After the holidays, he returned to school and the program with a lot of enthusiasm. His class choices for the spring semester were Outdoor Education & Recreation, Special Topics in ENV: The Idea of Nature, and Maps & Wilderness Navigation.

Louella and my friend went out to Prescott for the spring family conference of the Clean Adventures program. Unfortunately, Maria-Teresa could not get away from school.

The conference exposed families, as well as those with the addictions, to some of the underlying historical, emotional, and psychological factors that form a basis for development of and/or continuation of addictive behavior. It surprised your Grandfather that of the twenty or so families involved Sean's was the only one to have both his biological parents present.

Among other things during that weekend, the therapist tried to get Sean, Louella, and your Granddad to consciously experience the triangulation that characterized their relationships. For the afternoon, he suggested they NOT talk to one another directly. Rather, he wanted them to talk to each other through the third person of the triangle. As shared before, my friend quickly saw his own role in this unhealthy pattern. He later realized that they had failed to take full advantage of this exercise. As a result the lesson was lost to Louella and Sean. My friend had squandered an opportunity to address this dysfunctional and harmful communication which was so deeply entrenched.

In another part of the conference, one after another of the individuals and his family members would share their experiences. While each person's story was unique, they followed patterns. A number were not unlike the pattern and experiences of Sean, Louella, and your Granddad.

In that section of the program, several of the mothers confessed to enabling behavior toward their sons. Their pattern of behavior was essentially the same as Louella's. With the repetition, Louella seemed to develop awareness.

When the question of enabling came specifically to her, the therapist asked her if she was ready to change as a result of her new awareness. Did she believe she had enough insight and was she strong enough to stand up against Sean's drinking behavior? Then, to your Grandfather's amazement, as Louella sat wrestling with the very question central to her own behavior, the therapist stopped the program abruptly. He called for a lunch break.

My friend was stunned. The therapist had walked Louella to the point of awareness and decision -- only to stop just before she would commit.

Your Grandfather was astonished. He had, for years, witnessed Louella's enabling behavior toward Sean. He had worked for years to reach this crucial point in Louella's insight and growth. The therapist had walked her to this point of psychological awareness. Then he stopped short. That made absolutely no sense to Sean's Dad.

During the lunch break he confronted the therapist with the need to proceed. He got a commitment from the therapist to continue to work with Louella on this process after the lunch break.

Unfortunately, he would be astounded as the whole afternoon went by and no attempt was made by the therapist to honor that commitment.

Why? Your Granddad wondered.

He could only hope the therapist believed Louella had learned enough. She had committed to both Granddad and Sean to changing her role in Sean's addiction. She had come to the conference. She had heard the witness and the experiences of others.

Granddad knew she loved Sean. He had to imagine, with all that had happened, she would never resume her enabling ways nor contribute to Sean's addiction to alcohol.

The spring semester went as well or better than the fall semester had. Sean continued to be respectful, responsible, and hard-working. He seemed to grow in knowledge, understanding, and insight. He had adapted well.

Unfortunately, he still had the legal issues to deal with.

Chapter 25 -- THE SUMMER OF 2011. SEAN'S LAST
SUMMER

He was on probation for the 3rd DWI. And he had to report back personally and directly to the judge.

Clean Adventures, the therapeutic program, had been sending regular reports on Sean's progress to the judge through a probation officer.

Graciously, the judge had agreed to wait until summer to hold the hearing. That was done to allow Sean to complete the school year. It was now May, and time for Sean to face the judge once again.

Scheduling for the hearing was vague and uncertain. So, your Grandfather couldn't know for sure when to take off from work for the hearing. Thus, he decided not to go to the hearing. He knew how well Sean had done over the year. He knew the judge would be impressed. Your Granddad felt it more important to continue to work and save his vacation days to spend with Sean later, rather than go to court. My friend still saw his primary role as provider; provider of resources needed to support Sean's continued maturation and education.

Thus, your Grandfather was not there to witness the judge's praise. He was told later that the judge publicly proclaimed Sean's progress as a model of change and growth. Sean's Dad was delighted for and proud of his son. He knew with certainty such praise was warranted. And he also felt satisfied personally because such growth and change in Sean would not have been possible if he had not intervened on behalf of Sean almost 16 months earlier.

She, the judge, however, wanted Sean to serve the remaining 60 days or so for the probation violation. It was agreed he would do them in the form of "house arrest." He could do them during summer vacation and be able to get back to school in the fall.

My friend was told Sean would spend the time on "house arrest" at Louella's place. He was hurt and troubled by this. Despite the fact it was his efforts that had made all the progress possible, Sean would be staying not with him, but with his mother.

He tried to convince Sean to have this changed to his home instead Louella's. He explained his concerns to Sean.

Sean reasoned that by staying at his mother's place he would be closer to downtown Albuquerque, where he had to report, on a regular basis, for drug testing, Alcoholics Anonymous meetings, and counseling. His Father countered that transportation could be provided from Granddad's place and staying with his Dad would be good for both of them. But Sean had made up his mind. And Sean seemed to be both comfortable and confident in his decision.

As my friend was under the impression Sean had adequately progressed, as a result of therapy, he acquiesced. And, while hurt, because he would not get the time with Sean, he believed Sean had thought through his decision and would be safe. Too much had changed, over the 16 months, for Sean to slip backwards. How could anyone miss what a miraculous, life-altering transformation he had been through?

Shortly thereafter Sean began his sixty days.

The stipulations of "house arrest" would have allowed Sean to work. Unfortunately, his attempts at finding a job were unsuccessful. Several possibilities had excited Sean in the weeks before, but none worked out.

Your Grandfather was not surprised by this. He reasoned it was illogical for any prospective employer to hire Sean. Sean had no meaningful record of consistent, quality employment. And he was on "house arrest." Why choose Sean? Moreover, the country as a whole, at that time, was experiencing a job shortage due to the real-estate-bubble recession.

Consequently, and unfortunately, much of Sean's time on "house arrest" was wasted sitting in front of a television. He did have to report for the AA meetings and counseling multiple times over each week. And he had to be available for random drug testing. In addition he did some conscripted manual labor for the county. But mostly, he was biding his time, until he could return to Prescott.

His Dad never had reason to believe, or to suspect, Sean was drinking during this time of "house arrest."

It seemed to his Dad that Sean was still on the right track. From Louella's December 2009 request to help Sean through the spring of 2011, Sean had made tremendous progress. He was sober all that time. He had gone through extensive counseling and therapy. He was in college. He was positively enthusiastic and excited. He was being responsible. He was doing what he had to and what he should do to build a productive life for himself. My friend felt his prayers had been answered.

He saw Sean headed for success. And, as a result, he was more relaxed than he had been in a number of years.

It was during that time that another one of your Grandfather's prayers seemed to be answered.

In December, 2010, he met someone who was very out of the ordinary. She was similar to my friend in many ways. They began to spend more and more time together. They came to realize their values were very much aligned.

They prayed together. They shared their faith in God and in Christ.

They were both single and each preferred to have a partner. They considered marriage.

Over the first six months of 2011, they sought out advice and counseling.

They decided to get married.

As they made plans to formalize their commitment to one another, they wanted to pick a date that would work for both Sean and his sister, Maria-Teresa. After talking to both, they decided on August 27th. Sean would be off "house arrest" by then and he would not resume college until the following week. His sister would have already resumed her classes in Las Cruces, however she said she was OK with driving back up to Albuquerque for the weekend of August 27th.

Your Grandfather knew Sean hated to dress up. But Sean had worn a tuxedo for his cousin John's wedding years earlier, and Sean looked great in that tux. So, his Father offered to pay for a tux rental for Sean. Sean declined the offer. His Dad then offered to go shopping with Sean to pick out some nice clothes for the wedding. Sean agreed. They were to go after the end of "house arrest" and a few days before the wedding.

Curiously, in the days before they were to go, Sean sent a number of text messages to his Dad and to Cindy, Grandpa's fiancée, indicating that he, Sean, was unhappy about the wedding. Sean had not said anything in the months before. Why now? This seemed to be the old Sean. This seemed to my friend to be the kind of behavior Sean had exhibited during the years he was drinking. Sean was being indirect, accusatory, and negative.

The day came for Sean and Granddad to go shopping for the clothes. His Dad was to pick up Sean as he still had a revoked license and was prohibited from driving. An hour or so before the agreed upon pick-up time, Sean texted his Dad to cancel their shopping plans.

My friend was now concerned for his son. He decided to ignore the text and went over to see if Sean was OK. If he was there, then they could talk in person. If he wasn't there, then Granddad would leave him a note. It was a weekday and it was a logical presumption that Louella would be at work.

When your Grandfather arrived he heard very loud music
coming from the quarters. That did not make sense,
particularly given the hour of the day. It was early
afternoon. My friend was concerned about this disparity.
Something was not right.

He knocked.

No response.

He decided to try the door.

It opened.

He cautiously opened the door and put his head in.

There was a body sprawled on the couch. A young, male
body. Your Grandfather's first thought was that it was
Sean. His second thought was that he might be dead!

When a parent spends years worrying about an alcoholic,
drug-abusing child, the fear that some day that child might
die from intoxication is one of several nightmares that
recur.

He went in.

He looked closer.

It wasn't Sean. It was Sean's cousin, Patrick. And he was
breathing.

Thank God.

There was a whiskey bottle on the table. It was empty.

There were empty glasses.

And there was one last shot that had been poured, but not swallowed.

Grandpa turned the music down, thinking the quiet might stir up a response.   But there was no reaction.

He poured the remaining booze down the drain.   And he threw out the empty, one-liter bottle.

My friend looked around.   He found Sean lying down in the next room.

Sean stirred.   He mumbled that his Dad shouldn't be there.

Your Grandfather suggested to Sean that he get up and try to go with him.   Sean declined.   He was not interested.   He was tired.

Actually, he was drunk.

My friend felt sick.   A wave of nausea and disgust and disappointment welled up inside and enveloped him.

What to do?

At that time, there was nothing to be done.   Patrick and Sean were loaded.

He left.

And he thought.

Sean needed to get out of New Mexico and back to
Prescott. He needed to get away from temptations and
back to the supportive community that had nurtured him for
over a year. Clearly, that was what would be best for Sean.

The next day, your Granddad and Sean talked over the
phone. Sean declared that his Dad was somehow at fault
for coming over to see Sean. His Dad should have simply
accepted Sean's cancellation. It was his Dad who had
made a mistake.

My friend thought, Sean is back to the crazy thinking.
Sean drinks and acts irresponsibly and it is someone else's
fault. Sean made the bad decision to drink, and then
claimed it was his Dad's fault for discovering the lapse.

Your Grandfather encouraged Sean to return to Prescott
immediately.

He told Sean how he loved him. He told Sean it was more
important that he be sober and safe and back on track in
school and sobriety than be present at the wedding.

Sean said he understood and agreed.

He would leave in a day or two.

Chapter 26 -- THE RETURN TO PRESCOTT – SEAN'S LAST SIX MONTHS

Well, it turned out Sean didn't return to Prescott as discussed. But my friend was not told of the change in plans.

That Friday there was a dinner, the night before the wedding. This was to be for the wedding party, for close family (including Sean), and for guests who had come a long distance to share the weekend. As Granddad expected, Sean did not show up. So my friend continued to assume that his son had returned safely to Prescott as they had discussed.

It wasn't until the next day, just before the wedding itself, that your Grandfather realized that Sean had stayed in Albuquerque. Sean's Dad was shocked to see him at the church. Immediately, my friend was both concerned for his son and delighted to see him. Sean seemed to be sober.

Even as the wedding and the reception -- at which there was to be no alcohol -- proceeded, your Grandfather worried that Sean might relapse once again. That worry came because my friend knew that Sean had a number of cousins who drank rather freely. And that would make it much harder for Sean to abstain.

Your Grandfather could only hope for the best.

Fortunately, the day ended well. There were only five people left at the end of the reception: Sean; Maria-Teresa;

Granddad; his new wife, Cindy; and the minister who had that day married them. Together they sang a song of praise to God. The future looked hopeful for all of them.

A day or so later, Sean headed back to Prescott.

He had made arrangements to temporarily live at the vacation home of his mother's cousin there in Prescott. The positives: it would not cost him money and it was a place to put many of his things. The negative: the home was a few miles away from campus so he needed to commute back and forth. As he could not drive he would need to cycle.

Fortunately, Sean was in great physical condition. So the physical aspect of bicycling to and from campus was not going to be a problem. However, the time it would take to go back and forth and the inconvenience of having his things some distance away from school was going to be challenging.

His mom helped him to get a bicycle and drove him over to Prescott. She helped him to settle into his new quarters.

The semester was to start in only a few days. My friend assumed his son would be very busy with school work.

The fall classes were "Introduction to Rock Climbing", "Intermediate Rock Climbing", and "Concepts of Ecology."

Your Grandfather talked with Sean several times during the first few months of the school year. The bicycling was indeed a hassle. Coming in early some mornings, it was still cold. Going back late in the day, lugging his things was tedious.

Sean told the story of how a policeman stopped him one night. Sean was incredulous. What was he doing wrong? It seems that he was riding so fast that the policeman found him suspicious. Sean didn't care for police. But it turned out to be just an encounter, and a conversation piece in life.

Eventually, the hassle of living some distance from campus and bicycling took its toll. Sean began to stay in town at the places of various friends. Finally he moved into a tent in the back yard of some school mates. Despite sleeping outside, he would have access to kitchen and bathroom facilities. And he would be much closer to campus.

Sean came to love what he was learning about the outdoors. He would go out with friends at every opportunity: hiking, rock climbing, exploring.   Late in that semester, during the "student directed days", he went on a trip with friends to Fossil Creek, about an hour from Prescott. They were swimming, and jumping from a waterfall about 25 feet into a big pool. As he climbed back up to the top of the waterfall, he went by a different route, not the trail. One of the rocks he grabbed came loose and he tumbled about 30 feet into the water.

His compatriots, Sean later related, thought he might have died from the fall. They were happy to hear his moaning. He was scuffed up and injured. They rendered support, and considered options. They were so far out in the back country that their cell phones did not have coverage, and it was already very late in the day. They decided to wait until morning to head back to town. It was a few days before my friend was told what had happened.

Sean called his Dad to ask about his ribs. Sean was breathing OK and it was already several days since the injury. He was able to move about and get things done. He did not have a cough or a fever. He was not breathing abnormally, except for the pain. There was no real treatment to be recommended for a possible rib fracture; and, thus, no real benefit to be gained from an x-ray. An x-ray wouldn't change the treatment.

However, as they spoke your Granddad probed and learned about other injuries. As Sean described the fall it suggested an arm injury. When pressed, Sean confessed that he thought that he had dislocated his shoulder and that "they" had put it back in place the night of the fall. Your Grandfather was concerned about this. If indeed Sean had experienced a dislocated shoulder than he could suffer consequences for the rest of his life.

It was common for a once dislocated shoulder to be vulnerable as a result. It would be much easier to re-dislocate the joint. On the other hand, if the shoulder injury healed well, then the scarring could protect the joint and decrease the likelihood of recurrence.

As Sean was planning on making his living in large part by using his body, he would benefit greatly from a good, usable shoulder joint. His Father recommended that he see a doctor for evaluation. Initially, Sean agreed. However, when his Dad called to see how he was doing, the next day, he learned that Sean had balked. Sean claimed that he didn't have the money. My friend told his son that he would help with the medical expenses. Sean described that he was now able to use the shoulder, and that the pain was decreasing rapidly.

Your Grandfather then suggested that Sean work with a physical therapist. The best healing possible for the shoulder could come under the guidance of a top quality physical therapist. Your Granddad spent the afternoon, from his office in Albuquerque and in between caring for his own patients, shopping for a physical therapist for Sean in Prescott. He found someone who seemed very professional, knowledgeable, and accommodating.

Granddad called Sean back with the details. Sean agreed to set up the appointment.

Unfortunately, when my friend called back the next day Sean had not gone in. He explained that his school schedule, together with the hassle of physically getting to the office of the physical therapist, precluded his going. And, besides, he was feeling better.

All of this was consistent with Sean's behavior since his youth. Sean had always had a very high tolerance for physical pain. Even before he could walk, when he burned the back of his hand on a space heater, he only let out a slight whimper. And when he had broken his wrist in high school, your Granddad remembers Sean calmly walking up to his Father and matter-of-factly suggesting his wrist was broken as he demonstrated an obviously deformed distal forearm.

Sean could be stubborn and independent.

Thanksgiving came. And Sean was back in New Mexico. He was in good spirits and seemed confident and excited about his future. Granddad and Cindy enjoyed his company the evening after Thanksgiving. They shared a turkey day meal with Maria-Teresa. And they put up and decorated the Christmas tree.

They discussed Sean's life in Prescott and his future. Sean had decided on Adventure Education as his primary focus in school. It would be a wonderful mix of his talents and interests. Sean loved the outdoors and he had a passion for the high energy activities that adventure education encompassed.

As always, your Grandfather was very practical in his thinking. He quizzed Sean on the likelihood of finding meaningful employment when college ended. He reminded Sean that he would be finishing school with a considerable debt. Sean was fortunate in getting quite a bit of financial aid in the form of grants. Yet, he was also using loans to get his education. And Prescott College was not cheap.

Sean assured his Dad that there were jobs and that he was being responsible and reasonable about the future. He added that he hoped to have regular work, while at school, in the coming weeks.

Thanksgiving break was not long but he would finish the semester before Christmas and be off school for quite some time then. He talked of possibly taking a trip to Oregon with classmates to visit a friend and to do some rock climbing.

Soon Christmas came. Sean did not take the trip to Oregon. Rather, he considered a possible climb with friends in New Mexico instead.

Over the holidays he was busy visiting. He made time to spend with his Dad, but he lived or stayed at Louella's place. He shared a holiday get-together with his cousins on his dad's side of the family. All were impressed with the transformation in him. He was much more gregarious and self-assured. He had lots of positive things to share.

When he and his sister came over to share Christmas gifts and time with your Granddad and Cindy, he talked enthusiastically about rock climbing. He loved it.

Some weeks earlier he had called several times encouraging his Dad to watch a "You Tube" video of Alex Honnold free climbing Half Dome in Yosemite National Park. Now, at Christmas time, he claimed he was going to be able to do the same someday.

Cindy had picked up on his excitement and bought him for Christmas a DVD on climbing: "First Ascent: The Series." He was thrilled.

Then your Granddad talked with him about some of the details of climbing. After years of trying to help some patients live with the lifetime consequences of injuries and accidents, my friend wanted to know about the safety precautions in rock climbing. Logic told him how ropes and anchors can make peace with gravity and rock. But what about those who, for example, are above the anchors?

Given Sean's fall only weeks earlier, his Father assumed Sean had learned from the experience that his body could easily be broken. How could he not have learned?

Nonetheless, your Granddad was interested in specifics and wanted to share with Sean. What was Sean learning?

He asked specifically about how the lead climber, once above the highest anchor, is kept safe. Sean acknowledged that the lead climber was indeed above the best protection, but pointed out that he was still "roped up" and would be left hanging if he fell.

Your Granddad did the math with Sean. For each foot the leader climbed above the top anchor, the leader would -- or could -- fall that same many feet below the anchor should he tumble. From two feet above the anchor the fall would be four feet. From nine feet above the anchor the fall would be an eighteen foot fall.

Your Granddad sensed that Sean knew the risk but didn't grasp the potential magnitude. Sean seemed to discount his Father's concerns as overblown. Sean had been taught to do that.

My friend, after Sean's death, came to be haunted by this exchange with his son. Why hadn't he persisted in driving home the point he was trying to make with Sean? Why?

Sean headed back to Prescott with enthusiasm and excitement. His days were packed. In addition to school activities he would be working up to a score of hours each week. Steve Norrell, an upper classman, though Sean's junior in age, had started a landscaping business and was giving Sean a chance to earn.

His class for the month that started the semester was to be "Search and Rescue."

Chapter 27 -- JANUARY 18th, 2012, AM --THE
MORNING AFTER SEAN'S DEATH

They – your Grandfather, Louella, Cindy, and Maria-
Teresa -- were about to enter that same "Search and
Rescue" class, the morning of January 18th, as they stood
before the little shrine to Sean.

What was it in the shrine that had struck my friend so hard?

Mariah, you now have enough of the story to appreciate
what hurt Sean's Father as he looked at that shrine, and as
he went through the first two days after his son's death.

And you are close to understanding why your Granddad
came to believe your Dad didn't have to die.

The little shrine, the little memorial to Sean, was made up
of different things. It had cards, left by fellow students and
friends. The cards offered words to Sean and of Sean.

It had candles. They seemed to signify that, while the light
of Sean's life was over, flames of Sean's life still burned in
those he had touched.

There was a picture of Sean. The picture showed him full
of energy and enthusiasm -- full of life.

But the little shrine also had something else. Something
my friend was not expecting.

It had a row of cans and "miniatures". Beer cans and miniature alcohol bottles.

Your Granddad was stunned.

Maybe he should not have been. But he was.

My friend immediately realized what those meant.

They meant Sean had been drinking again. And not just a little bit. And not just once in a while.

Those were signs from "drinking buddies."

Sean had resumed his drinking.

Friends don't leave those kinds of things at a memorial if they have been helping a guy to stay sober.

Your Grandfather's stomach dropped. He felt sick. A wave of emotions came over him.

Disappointment.

Frustration.

Resentment.

Exasperation.

Dejection.

He had thought Sean's war with alcohol had been won.

But he didn't say anything. Who could he share these thoughts and feelings with? Almost immediately, as they stood there at the shrine, students were stopping by. They were mourning and remembering Sean. They were trying their best to share and to accept Sean's life -- and his death.

How could anyone else understand what was going on inside of my friend?

He felt alone, even as he shared with others. He sensed that there was no one -- no one else but him -- who knew of all Sean had struggled with. And for so long.

Except...

Except, maybe, Louella.

Maybe Louella was as surprised as he was. Maybe she saw the alcohol containers and knew what they represented.

Over the past year and a half, she had grown in her understanding. By now she had a better knowledge and appreciation of what Sean had battled for years.

Maybe she felt the same things Sean's Dad was feeling.

But before he could find out, or even fully process what he had just learned from the shrine, he was hit by the second of the three blows he would receive that day.

Several young men, fellow students and friends of Sean, came up. When they realized who your Grandfather and the others were, they began sharing their thoughts and experiences of Sean. They told how energetic and enthusiastic he was. They described how happy he had been, for months. Matter-of-factly, they mentioned how proud Sean was to be saving money for his daughter, and how he was planning for his future.

Your Grandfather's brain stopped. Had he heard correctly?

A daughter?

Louella and Maria-Teresa didn't seem surprised.

Cindy would know nothing of Sean having a daughter.

A daughter?

Now his head and his heart churned even more.

What was the reality?

What was the truth?

If Sean had a daughter, how was it that his Father, who had sacrificed so much to help Sean, didn't know of this?

Sinking sickness.

A feeling of sinking sickness filled him.

Sean was dead.

Sean had not been soberly living his life.

And Sean had left behind a daughter?

Truth…

Where was truth?

What was the truth?

How could these things be true?

That was the mix he carried as he went upstairs and into the classroom. The mix of questions and thoughts, of feeling and emotions.

The five of them went in. The four of them and the Dean.

The students had already started. Long tables had been placed to form a square. The chairs to the outside of the square. Each could see all the others.

Some of the students stood up and offered their chairs. The four of them sat. The dean remained standing.

Quiet. An expectant quiet.

Faculty and students were probably waiting to see how the four of them were doing.

The quiet was not for long.

Soon they learned that most of the young adults who had been with Sean the day before were present, this morning, in this very class.

Your Grandfather, Louella, Maria-Teresa, and Cindy wanted to know what had happened. And they wanted to know how the young folks were doing.

Some of the details were shared.

Feelings and thoughts were shared.

Questions were raised.

And even as your Granddad and the others shared, his mind and his heart were trying to make sense of what he had just learned before coming to the classroom.

Why was he so surprised to learn that Sean was again drinking? How could he have assumed Sean was living sober?

In the midst of his anguish and grief, he was angry.

Angry at himself.

How stupid he was. How naïve.

To think that Sean had stopped drinking.

And he was hurt.

Why had he not been told of a child? Why did he have to learn such a thing in this manner? At this time?

A decision was made to go out to the site where Sean had died. The "Search and Rescue" instructor had been told where it was, and they would drive out here that morning.

Then they would return and have lunch with classmates, friends, and faculty at "The Commons".

It turned out that the place they went to that morning was close to but not the exact site. That afternoon, they would return and see exactly where the fall occurred.

At noon, they visited with others as planned.

My friend was delighted to hear how his son had been a positive person in so many others' lives. He seemed to have many friends. It seems that he was upbeat and positive with everyone. Each had stories to share. Sean was a unique guy with a knack for fun.

Granddad heard once again about this daughter. Seems Sean had shared with a number of his friends how he was working for and planning to take care of her. Your Grandfather listened. Amazed. Full of mixed feelings. He was proud of Sean for taking on responsibilities. He was hurt that he had been deceived. He wondered about this child whom he had never met.

Several of Sean's friends invited the four of them to join them that evening. They were going to Coyote Joe's, a drinking establishment or "watering hole" in town. Where was it? What time? Louella shared that she knew the place. She had been there with Sean.

Boom. The third blow.

Louella had been to Coyote Joe's with Sean.

Your Granddad had gone to college. He had gone to his share of parties. He had done his share of drinking in college. He had gone to his share of "watering holes." He understood the lingo and the "way of being" these young folks were sharing, describing, and inviting them to join in. He knew what it meant when Louella responded as she did.

Louella had been to Coyote Joe's with Sean, and with some of his friends. And they had all been drinking together.

My friend said nothing. He was too stunned.

Not only was Sean drinking again; not only was his mother aware of that; but she was actively participating in his drinking!

Your Grandfather felt as if he had been hit in the gut.

He said nothing.

Later, in the car he asked about plans for the evening. Again, Louella shared her awareness of Coyote Joe's and how she had been there a number of times.

She had been there a number of times.

It wasn't just once.

If Coyote Joe's was a number of times, it was certain that the drinking together – Sean and Louella – was not limited to Coyote Joe's.

She had betrayed him.

Louella had lied to your Grandfather.

All the time and effort and money and people that had been brought to bear in helping Sean to overcome his alcoholism had been ripped asunder by Louella. His mother had not only failed to learn her role in Sean's alcoholism; she had not only resumed her "enabling" behavior; but she had become his drinking partner.

How could she?

What was she thinking? Or, not thinking.

My friend couldn't believe what he was hearing.

Your Grandfather could not grasp what he was experiencing.

Sean was dead.

Sean had resumed drinking.

Sean had a daughter.

Louella was Sean's drinking partner.

Chapter 28 -- JANUARY 18, 2012, PM – THE AFTERNOON AND EVENING AFTER SEAN'S DEATH

Sean's Dad had learned the evening before that his son's body had been taken to the Yavapai County Medical Examiner's office, because he had died in an accident. Your Granddad assumed they would complete their examination and release his body later the same day. When the four of them arrived back at the campus after the initial trip to Granite Dells, and before they went to lunch, he called the Medical Examiner's office. He was told the examination would not be carried out for two or three more days.

He was furious. What did they need to do? The cause of his death was obvious. The family was ready to take his body. What could be done to move the process along?

Joseph, of the examiner's office, would see what he could do and call him back.

They headed for lunch.

During the meal and the sharing, at the Commons, it became apparent to students and faculty that the four of them had not seen the actual site of Sean's fall. Students who had been with Sean the day before were now interested in returning and showing the correct place to the family.

They went back out to Granite Dells. They hiked up and around to the south side of a prominent formation.

It was a chance to share. Yet it was painful. Even as he learned more about the fall itself, my friend's thoughts and emotions still reeled from the things he had learned during the past six hours.

Then they saw his blood. The blood from Sean's head wound still stained the rock where the blow occurred. They saw where he lay for probably an hour or more as he died.

Why did it happen? What, again, were the details? Who was where at the time of the fall?

My friend had the ear and the attention of the teacher of the Search and Rescue class, Phil Latham, an experienced climber. He reviewed with Phil what he was hearing and came to realize that the fall was not an accident. The fall was a mistake. Actually, it was the result of a number of mistakes. At least five.

Your Grandfather would go over this sequence again and again in the coming days.

Each time he reached the same conclusion.

They all drove back in a caravan of cars to the Prescott College campus. There was no rushing. It seemed to him all was in slow motion or that there was an odd leisure in the flow. That slowing of life was to continue in him for days -- and to recur in him possibly forever.

It was now late afternoon and the school was holding a gathering on Sean's behalf. It was held in a meeting room in the Mariposa Building on Grove Avenue.

The large room was filled with chairs arranged in a big circle. Sean's Dad was stunned by the number of people present. There were at least eighty people, maybe a hundred. The chairs were filled. A few stood outside the circle.

Your Grandfather was deeply moved by their presence. Good people. Taking time from their busy day to honor his son.

So many years of Sean's life had been with other troubled souls. People who were not busy with good things to do. The kind who were not likely to show up when trouble -- or even death – came.

It could have been so different. He could have died in an auto accident while drunk. He could have caused the death of others. He could have been trapped in prison.

And, on the other hand, he could **not** have made those mistakes. He could still be alive.

One after another, from different spots in the circle, individuals spoke of Sean. Many had close relationships with him. Many more than his Dad would have guessed. Others were acquaintances or friends of friends. And there were teachers and administrators who knew him or knew of him. Each had kind or favorable words to share.

A number of the speakers pointed out that Sean had many more friends and acquaintances who could not be present. Those individuals were taking classes far from the main campus. They would surely have come to the gathering, if they could have.

Classes at Prescott College are small. So there was much more personal interaction within each class. Special relationships had been forged. In some ways, Prescott College was the kind of community Sean had needed. Sean's Dad saw what he thought of as a blessing in having found this school for Sean.

There was a theme in the experiences that those people shared. Sean was energetic, outgoing, hard-working, and full of life. My friend couldn't get over the number of individuals who shared sincere, personal, and very positive stories of Sean. How had Sean been able to pack so much into his days in Prescott?

The words of these people warmed your Grandfather's heart. Yet at the same time he was jealous of those experiences. They were the kind of sharing with Sean that was just being rekindled in his relationship with his son. He was so looking forward to his future with Sean.

Not to be.

As the gathering closed, the four of them lingered. Afternoon was beginning to turn to evening. They had gotten little if any sleep the night before. They had not planned on spending the night in Prescott. Now, it seemed that spending more time in Prescott was appropriate and necessary. They wanted to continue to share with Sean's friends, and they would need time to gather his belongings.

As they spoke, a student came up. Rachel Young. She heard their discussion and offered them a place to stay for the evening.   She explained that many of her housemates were among those taking the month-long semester class away from campus.   There were open beds.

It seemed reasonable to take her up on the offer, and it would greatly simplify the evening, and the next day.

They went over to the house on North Willow, near the campus.   The dropped off their things and freshened up.

Sean had purchased some brisket and had planned to make a community meal with it.   Several of his friends and roommates would honor him and his plan, and they invited the four of them over to share in the meal.   They went over to share Sean's brisket.

It was early evening, but not yet dark, when they arrived at the house on Campbell Street.   They were offered drink when they arrived.   Louella and Maria-Teresa readily accepted alcoholic beverages.   In light of all that transpired over the day, over the months, over the years, my friend felt dismayed at the choice to drink alcohol – Sean's arch-enemy.

Louella's choice to drink reinforced what he then still hoped was an erroneous assumption on his part.   He was filled with disappointment and anguish.   He was deeply pained.   His alcoholic son was being mourned and remembered by his closest relatives over a drink!   The central problem of alcohol in Sean's life, which my friend thought had been overcome, continued to so permeate the family that this drinking behavior seemed normal.

They visited and shared with the students and friends. The atmosphere was warm and caring. The affection for Sean was palpable.

However the 24 hours had taken its toll and by 8 pm, your Grandfather's body thought it was after 10. He and Cindy realized that this college evening was going to linger, with more and more alcohol. What good would come from more of that? They decided to bow out and go back and rest. Louella and Maria-Teresa would stay and find a ride back to the house on North Willow.

Later that night he woke as Louella and Maria-Teresa came in. They were chattering.

Then he heard the wrenching -- and the retching. Maria-Teresa was sick. The effects of alcohol continued.

Why?

He laid there listening through the thin walls.

Why drink so much? What good was coming from it? Had they not seen and experienced enough? Had they not seen how alcohol kept Sean from his life? Could they not see the major role addiction had in ripping the family apart? Why were they drinking? And worse, why drinking to excess?

Is this the choice God wanted to be made?

And where was God?

Your Grandfather Michael had, repeatedly, over the years, prayed and prayed.

"What good had it done?" he now asked himself.

As he lay there, my friend had a deep sense of his failure and sin. Sure he had prayed, but the prayers had not borne fruit.

Sean had not overcome alcohol. He had resumed his drinking.

Louella had not changed. Rather than give up her enabling she did the very opposite, she had joined Sean in his alcoholism.

Now his daughter, Maria-Teresa, was grieving her brother's death and heaving from alcohol, only hours after Sean's death.

Where was the good fruit?

By any simple calculation, he had failed as the head of a household.

At the very minimum a father should be able to protect his children. He had not done so.

He lay there not sleeping, but rather mourning and remembering.

What could he have done differently? What should he have done differently?

What should he now do?

If his life had not borne fruit, his life had not been blessed.

The prayers he had made had not come to goodness. Did he even know how to pray? Wasn't he selfish, just like most others?

Clearly, he had not had the patience and the faith of Hosea.

Would that have changed things? Would Sean still be alive if he had?

What kind of a family, what kind of relationship, can be built on deception? None of the three of them had told him of this granddaughter. Not Louella. Not Maria-Teresa. Not Sean.

Why?

He continued to wrestle with these things. He continued to battle within.

Then, sometime later...   minutes...   maybe an hour, he heard the mumblings.

Then the crying.

Then the moaning.

Then the wailing.

Of grief...

Of grief being poured out.

It was Louella.

Crying for her son.

It was also Maria-Teresa.

She was crying for her brother. And she seemed also to be crying for her mother's grief as well.

He had not been able to protect his family.

Through the thin walls of this house on North Willow Street in Prescott, Arizona, he heard a human sorrow spilling out that no father or husband is ever prepared to hear.

As it went on, he was overwhelmed by their pain.

He made his way into the room the two of them shared. They were wrapped in each other's arms. Sobbing.

He joined them.

The three of them lay there.

Joined in their sorrow.

Crying.

Holding each other.

Would that it were not so.

If only Sean were still alive?

Chapter 29 -- JANUARY 19, 2012

Eventually the night ended.

Rachel was gracious and made breakfast for them all. Eggs and peppers.

And she shared with them. Among other things she proffered that there wasn't a girl at Prescott College who didn't find Sean attractive.

Then each began to wash up.

Things still seemed to be moving slowly, delicately, steadily.

Your Granddad touched base again with the Medical Examiner's office. They had called him back at some point the afternoon before to say that they would move the examination of Sean's body to today, January 19th. He wanted to know when they would be able to release the body. They told him the exam would start early in the afternoon. It could be released late that afternoon.

As the others were preparing for the day, your Granddad called Phil Latham and set up a meeting. Among all his other thoughts, your Granddad kept reviewing the events of Sean's death. He wanted to talk again, with Phil, to be sure of his understanding of those events.

And, with Rachel's help, he found a credit union, two
blocks away, on Grove and West Gurley, as he needed
cash.

An 11 am meeting pushed them out of the house. It was at
the business office of Prescott College; to deal with Sean's
school loans and associated paper work.

My friend again found the people of the college more
gracious than he could have imagined. They had, already
that morning, dismissed Sean's tuition for the semester and
had contacted the lending entities to notify them of Sean's
death. All of his loans were to be written off. Only some
formalities of paperwork did they have to deal with.

They went from the business office a few blocks over to the
school's San Juan building on Garden Street for your
Grandfather's meeting with Phil. That building served
many purposes for the school.

There they saw the large equipment warehouse from which
the various pieces of equipment for outdoor classes were
dispensed to students. Granddad remembered how, less
than a year earlier, Sean had shown him this place with all
the excitement of his enthusiasm for the outdoors.

The student's mailroom was also there. They had a few
pieces of Sean's mail.

Some faculty offices were upstairs. It was there that he
talked with Mr. Latham. My friend again reviewed his
understanding of the events and the decisions on the rocks

two days earlier. Phil agreed that there were a series of miscalculations. One that was painfully obvious to everyone was that none of the climbers were wearing their helmets.

There was a gracious parting and a sharing of respect. Another person from the college had most kindly given of his time.

The four of them decided to go to lunch before heading to Sean's storage unit. They settled on a place called Sue Ann's Apple Pan, on West Gurley near North Summit. They got a table near the window, looking out on another beautiful, sunny, Prescott day.

After each of the four had placed an order, my friend asked a simple, open-ended question, "What's this about a little girl?"

This was the first that any words passed among them regarding Sean and a child. Cindy expressed her surprise at such news. Of course, she would. How would she know, if her husband hadn't? They did not keep such important matters from one another.

Louella and Maria-Teresa shared that they knew of the little girl.

My friend told of his shock the morning before when Sean's friends had mentioned how dedicated Sean was to his daughter. And again his sense of being rendered speechless when they had all heard similar comments from Sean's friends at the large gathering the afternoon before.

Your Grandfather was calm and the atmosphere at the table was cordial. Yet neither Louella nor his daughter expressed any empathy for what he might be feeling under the circumstances. He wondered the obvious "How would they have felt if placed in his position?" He was simply asking for their understanding and compassion. But those were things that could not be demanded, they could only be allowed. He wanted to allow them. They refused. Neither one of them expressed any understanding for his position or sympathy for his feelings. He was deeply hurt and disappointed at their lack of compassion.

Louella took a defensive attitude. As always, he thought, self-centered. She stated that it was Sean who was to have told his Father. She deflected any responsibility onto Sean. She understood that Sean had planned to tell his Dad over the Christmas holidays. But, apparently, she also knew that he had not done so.

Why? Why had Louella not intervened? How would she have felt and responded if the tables had been turned and she had been left out of such an important part of her life?

Neither Louella nor Maria-Teresa expressed any responsibility for -- or any regret for -- the failure to inform him that he was thought to be a Grandfather. There is a dark coldness in the hearts of some.

My friend then asked other important and appropriate questions.

How old was the child?
How long had Sean and Louella and Maria-Teresa known?
Who was the mother?
How was the little girl?
Where did she live?

What was her name?

She was four years old.
Sean knew since Thanksgiving. Louella and Maria-Teresa
knew since, at least, Christmas.
The mother was Rina. She was in jail!
The girl was healthy and happy.
She lived in Albuquerque.
Her name was Mariah.

So was this the same child Louella had mentioned as being
expected when Sean was headed for treatment four years
earlier?
If she was four years old, how was it that they had only
been aware of her since Thanksgiving at the earliest?
Why was her mother in jail?
Who was caring for her?
Where in Albuquerque did she live?

She was the same child of four years earlier.
They were vague, or not forthcoming, about why
knowledge of her had been only since Thanksgiving.
Mom was in jail for issues related somehow to drugs.
The child's maternal grandmother was caring for her.
Child and grandmother lived on the west side of
Albuquerque. Louella and Maria-Teresa had been to their
house.

Granddad reminded Louella that she had told him two
years earlier that the child expected four years ago had
turned out **not** to be Sean's child. What was the truth?
What happened to change that?
Was everyone certain the child is Sean's?
Did the grandmother have legal custody?

What were the plans for the little girl?

Louella could not or would not give a clear answer regarding the sequence of events over the four years. He was told that the little girl's maternal grandmother, Sean, and Louella all believed the child to be Sean's. However, paternity testing had never been carried out. Louella believed the grandmother had some form of legal custody.
Sean was assuming, as his friends had related the day before, as much responsibility for the child as he could.

Your Grandfather made a mental review: Sean's assumed responsibilities for this little girl explained why Sean was working so hard while in school to make money and still asking for and accepting his Father's money.

Whew!

What to do?

My friend's head was spinning.

He tried to get his thoughts around what was being presented together with the possibilities and the proper actions to take.

If he was a Grandfather, he had certain responsibilities -- morally if not legally -- to the little girl.

And...

And even as he thought of those, other decisions and actions had to be made -- and carried out.

How would they get Sean's body from the medical examiner's office to New Mexico?
Where would the funeral be held?
What funeral parlor?
When?
A funeral Mass needed to be planned.

Why had he not been told of a child? What had he done – or not done – that such an important relationship would be kept from him?

My friend knew that no one else could have or would have created the opportunity that he had for his son. Who else put together the circumstances that allowed Sean to heal, to grow up, to develop his talents, and to overcome his obstacles?

And yet, Sean – and others – had continued to deceive him.

Sure he was hurt. Hurt and disappointed.

How could the sick and twisted relationships have continued? Here he was, trying to come to terms with his son's death, and yet he found himself still experiencing the deception and dysfunction that characterized the dynamics when Sean was alive.

No paternity testing had been done, and Sean's body would soon be buried. "What now needed to be done?" he asked.

He learned from Louella that paternity testing had been discussed at some point in the past. The child's mother had refused. Louella felt the child's grandmother would be agreeable to such testing. Apparently there was a laboratory in Albuquerque that did such testing. Could they do such testing now, he wondered aloud?

Your Grandfather, as a doctor, had been involved in postmortem examinations as part of his training. He felt the medical examiner could get some blood from Sean's body at the exam, if they acted fast. The exam was going on even as they sat there. And Sean's body had to be embalmed before it would be allowed to leave Arizona for New Mexico.

He called the Albuquerque lab. Amazingly, that laboratory was closed for that particular week only!

Your Granddad had just obtained a new "smart phone". He didn't know how to use all the functions, but Maria-Teresa was able to use it to get crucial information. As a result he was able to reach a national laboratory that specialized in paternity testing.

The representative of that lab was very professional, informative, and confident. He was able to answer all of the crucial questions regarding legality and handling of specimens. He was convinced they could work with the medical examiner's office and get the needed sample that day.

Your Granddad called the medical examiner's office and Joseph, the office's representative, agreed to work with the lab. With a down payment from your Granddad's credit card to the lab, he was able to start the process.

Louella and Sean's Dad then agreed on Espanola as the location for the funeral. A funeral home there was called and would arrange for Sean's body to be picked up, embalmed in Arizona, and transported. Louella and your Granddad would work on arrangements for the funeral Mass when they got back to New Mexico.

Much had happened during those two hours at Sue Ann's Apple Pan. And some things didn't happen. Most notably for my friend: there was no empathy shared and no apologies offered by Louella or by his daughter.

They went to Sean's storage unit. Louella knew where it was. She had access. There were not many things in the unit. She knew which ones were Sean's and which ones belonged to his friend.

Then they headed to the house Sean shared with others. They picked up his things. Ali, his friend, had laundered Sean's clothes. She, and the others, would deeply miss him.

Sean's things were all separated and organized. Most things would fit into the back of the pickup truck. Some would be brought to New Mexico by his friends, as a number of them were coming to his funeral.

They said good-byes and went back to Rachel's place on North Willow Street for their own things.

All items had to be secured in the back of the pickup, which was open to the elements. And getting the tarp to cover and the straps tight and affixed to the sides was more of a time-consuming hassle than anticipated. Eventually, they were prepared and on the road back to Albuquerque.

Chapter 30 -- STARTING BACK TO ALBUQUERQUE; LOOKING BACK TO SEAN'S BEGINNINGS

Driving back to Albuquerque, my friend had lots on his mind and hours of time to reflect.

His mind went back to Sean's beginnings.

When your Dad was very young, there was a time before conflict. But gradually and most certainly the atmosphere within the marriage changed.

Your Granddad, before he married Louella, had a positive, can-do, loving, and caring attitude toward life.

He brought that into the marriage.

However, by the time Sean was in high school the tone had changed completely. The tone was pessimistic, must-do, fearful, and conflicted.

What had happened? And, why?

Six years before your Dad was born, his Father, fresh out of specialty training at the University of New Mexico, went to the town of Espanola, New Mexico, to establish a medical practice. He did so with a partner named Margaret McCreery, with whom he had done his last two years of residency training at UNM. They worked hard and struggled together those six years.

222

But we have to go back even further for you to understand some of the other things that happened. Things that came to affect your Dad: Sean, my friend's son.

Five years before settling in Espanola, my friend had come to the sense that God wanted him to go to Northern New Mexico to work with the poor in this disadvantaged, yet physically beautiful, area. Several of the counties in Northern New Mexico were among the poorest in the state. And New Mexico was one of the poorest states in the Union. That made, of course, the area around Espanola one of the poorest in the United States.

Once he had felt that "calling" he poured himself into preparing. He worked hard over those five years. He learned about the history and the culture of the area. He studied the language and even the folk remedies of the Hispanic population. Of course, this was all done even as he worked his way through medical school and did residency training in the medical specialty of Family Practice. He did his best to prepare himself to serve patients in Northern New Mexico.

He arrived in Espanola after completing training with that positive, can-do, loving, and caring attitude I mentioned above.

In his first six years there, he and Dr. McCreery not only started their practice in Espanola, but also tried to help in the more rural areas surrounding Espanola. They "backed up" the clinic in Truchas, New Mexico, which served small

223

towns or villages to the east. They also "backed up" the clinic in Chama, New Mexico, some 90 miles northwest of Espanola.

They did many other positive things for the people of the area.

Here is one small example: Your Granddad had worked in Tierra Amarilla, which is located maybe 60 miles north of Espanola and 30 miles south of Chama, New Mexico. He did this for three intense weeks three years before settling in Espanola. That was just after he finished medical school and before he started his residency. He drove out from his home state of Missouri to volunteer his medical knowledge at the "free" community clinic in TA.

The community of Chama also had a clinic. The clinic in Tierra Amarilla and the Chama clinic saw themselves as competitors, for cultural and historic reasons. Later, when he had settled in Espanola and was "back up" physician to the clinic in Chama, your Grandfather had personal contacts at both clinics. Through those contacts he played a quiet but effective role in bringing those competitors together. They began to share instead of competing. And, as a result, the limited resources of these rural and relatively poor communities were made available to more people.

During those first six years in Espanola your Grandfather was still a single man. He and Dr. McCreery, as I said, both worked very hard. They each put in over 60 hours every week caring for patients as well as trying to run the business aspects of a medical office.

On the clinical -- or medical -- side there was both office work and hospital work to be done. They cared for children and adults both outside and inside of the hospital. The hospital work included, in addition to patients on the wards, patients in the intensive care unit, assisting with surgeries, and delivering babies. It was a time before a number of the medical advances we now have. There were no ultrasounds or vascular stents, no MRIs and no laparoscopic surgery.

Despite the long hours of work each week, your Granddad would often get up early to do spiritual reading and to seek God's help and blessing. He also did his best to find time to go to Catholic Mass several days during the week, in addition to Sunday Mass.

He tried to make time for some exercise and a social life.

However, he did not put as much detailed thought or preparation into getting ready for marriage and family life as he had for medicine. His background and upbringing led him to make a number of assumptions about marriage and about raising children. These assumptions he thought were reasonable[5]. It was only later he came to realize they were rather naive. These mistaken assumptions – regarding fatherhood and marriage -- would prove to be critically harmful to himself and his family, particularly to his son, Sean.

As he drove back from Prescott that night, he looked back to the year he and Louella married. Decisions were made at that time which shaped Sean's life.

---

[5] But isn't that what we all do with assumptions: consider them reasonable?

The biggest decision, of course, was to marry and have a
child. That child was your Dad: Sean.

The second big decision was actually the result of a choice
neither of them made. Just before your Dad's birth, your
Granddad's partner, Dr. McCreery, decided to leave
Espanola. That left him with a dilemma. He and Dr.
McCreery, only the year before -- and after five years of
hard work -- had settled into a building that was to be their
own. With his partner's departure he was left with a big
question. Should he move out of the building and give it
up, or should he try to continue on his own in the building
(assuming the entire mortgage alone) and while looking for
a new partner?

Being still an optimist and a hard worker, he envisioned a
positive outcome. He envisioned finding another partner.
And he thought his new wife would soon ease the burden
of administering the business aspects of the private medical
practice. So, he decided to stay in the building and add his
partner's share of the mortgage to his financial
responsibilities.

His plan and his thinking went like this. He would
temporarily increase his clinical work, and -- thus -- the
billings of the practice. He would do that first to pay for the
overhead previously paid through the work of two doctors
and second to keep the patient volume up, so as to have
enough work to attract another doctor. This resulted in a
substantial increase in hours worked. With Dr. McCreery
he had been working a little over 60 hours per week, but he
had Thursdays off and he was "on call" for emergencies,
deliveries of babies, and hospital work only 50% of the
time. After her departure and for the time being, he would
add all day on Thursdays and take all the "call" (24 hours

226

per day, 7 days a week) -- until he could get additional help. Thus, he would be working over 85 hours per week.

 The third big decision had to do with the house. Shortly before he and Louella met, your Grandfather had taken out a mortgage on a small adobe house. It was OK for a single guy, or even a married couple, but not for a family. He would need a larger house to raise a family. He and Louella decided to remodel and add on. He had a good friend who was experienced in construction and willing to help.

These three decisions placed an extremely heavy burden on my friend. The most significant consequences of these decisions were invisible to others: spiritual consequences. He was giving up his habit of morning prayer and spiritual reading. And he lost the little time he had had for more frequent Mass attendance.

The end result of these decisions and their consequences would include the loss of his youthful energy and play a role in the loss of his optimism

 It was only in retrospect he saw how these choices–combined with his mistaken assumptions -- drained him completely of personal free time, and also drained him of his caring and can-do attitude. Ever since the year of Sean's birth he was sapped of time and energy that should have gone to his family, including his son, Sean.

He and Louella had dated for almost four years before marriage. They had had plenty of time to talk about things.

By the time they married Louella had finished three years of college. She was majoring in business administration. As mentioned above, your Grandfather imagined that when she finished school she would be able to manage the business side of the medical practice, relieving him of that burden.

With Sean to be born in October, they decided Louella should take a year off of school to be available to Sean, both physically and emotionally. She would return to college the following year, and gain her degree.

However, during that year -- the first year of their marriage -- he came to realize she would not be capable of taking on the business and administrative responsibilities at the medical office as he had envisioned. That burden was never to be lifted from him.

On a positive note, it wasn't long after Dr. McCreery's departure that a collaborating physician joined the medical practice. With her arrival my friend was able to cut back a bit on his clinical work. He no longer had to see patients on Thursdays. And some of the hospital work was shared with this doctor, and thus decreased for him. However, and unfortunately, the new physician was not a specialist as was your Grandfather. So, she could not deliver babies, nor did she have privileges in the intensive care unit. Thus, he continued to be under the constant pressure "call" 24 hours per day, seven days a week, for the obstetrical patients and the intensive care unit work.

As mentioned, Louella was never able to manage the business of the practice. So – although he was free of clinical work on Thursdays – he still went into work each Thursday to handle those responsibilities. Down from about 85 hours per week of work within the medical practice to maybe 75 hours per week of such work.

The remodeling of the house went well, but very slowly. They decided to take on no more debt to modernize the house and put on an addition. So they had to pace themselves as cash flow allowed. And, because much of the work was coordinated and drawn up (literally, the "blueprints") by your Grandfather, it was an additional consumption of his time. Indeed, five years later, when the family moved to Las Vegas, Nevada, the work was still not quite completed. The new kitchen (to be within the new addition), as well as an additional bathroom, were not finished.

Decisions and assumptions, he pondered. Assumptions and decisions that shaped -- and were shaped by -- the relationship between your Grandfather and Louella. It was that relationship within which Sean would develop.

On this drive back to Albuquerque, two nights after your Dad's death, my friend thought about that relationship. Over the years he had come to realize that his image of – and thus his assumptions about -- a wife was more hope than reality.

He and Louella had shared a Catholic faith. He had gone to Catholic schools from kindergarten thru college. He believed that the values with which he grew up were fundamental to Catholicism. He thought that their shared

229

Catholicism gave them a common foundation of shared values. Not so, it turned out.

And his assumptions about marriage affected his assumptions about fatherhood. He thought being a good father meant being a good provider for his family. He expected, as a father, to participate some in the discipline and direction of his children. But he presumed their mother would be home much more than he and would be the primary teacher and guide to the children. That is what he grew up with.

He presumed hard work and absolute honesty in marriage. And it never crossed his mind that anyone would not cherish education or would not be willing to sacrifice for the best schools. He also assumed his marriage would be between two equal and collaborating partners.

He had worked very hard and forfeited much for his education. He did this in large part so that any future spouse might not be obliged to work outside the home, though she could freely choose to do so. He took for granted a wife who would fully understand and appreciate the sacrifices he had made. And he expected a wife who would manage the house and the household effectively, efficiently, and with joy.

Above all, he looked forward to being loved, honored, and cherished by his wife. And he assumed she would expect the same attitude from her children toward their father, her husband. Why would anyone marry him if she didn't care deeply for him and about him?

All those assumptions seemed reasonable to him. However, in reality, they all turned out to be limited, flawed, or downright erroneous. Married life didn't turn out as he had assumed.

Early in the marriage, some aspects of their life together and of shared child rearing were fun and full of joy. But, little by little, over the years, he became aware of significant differences between himself and Louella.

Along the way, when awareness of a disparity arose, your Granddad would talk with his wife about it. He would believe that they had talked things through to a mutual understanding. He would then consider the problem or the difference changed, resolved, or passed. Sometimes that is how things turned out. But other times issues would simply recur.

Eventually, it became clear to him that Louella was telling him what he wanted to hear, even if it was not the truth. This fundamentally undermined the relationship. Without consistent honesty, he didn't know when she was being truthful and when she was simply placating him. Without trust, how could partnership and co-parenting be realized?

For reasons that now made no sense to him he had thought that when he entered into the agreement with Louella to help Sean, in December 2009, the placating and deception would end. There never was a good reason to lie. Even less so if they were working together to help Sean.

On this drive back to Albuquerque, the most recent deceptions churned within him. He had to admit his error. He had quixotically held onto a hope that she would change. And he had to admit to himself that this flawed hope – as well as his over-optimistic decisions and mistaken assumptions – all contributed to Sean's challenges and difficulties. All the way to the end.

Chapter 31 -- A SIMPLE QUESTION; DECEPTION; NAIVETE; AND THE REALITY OF BETRAYAL

My friend felt that when he and Louella agreed in early 2010 to help Sean, the long sought changes could occur.

Three family conferences and dramatic changes in Sean during 2010 and 2011 led him to believe his hope had been realized. That the dysfunction was dissipating.

They had been on the road about three hours and now it was about one in the morning. They were about half way back to Albuquerque. Your Grandfather was driving. Maria-Teresa was half asleep in the seat behind her father with Cindy also in the back seat, on the other side, fast asleep. Louella was seated in the front on the passenger's side.

My friend's mind continued to wrestle with the past, the events of the last few days, and the reality of his son's death.

The question came to him simply enough. And, as Louella was awake, he verbalized it, as much thinking out loud as out of curiosity. "Louella," he asked, "how do you wrap your mind around drinking with Sean? How do you make sense out that?"

She didn't hear the tone of curiosity. He remembers her response to be something along the lines of "Don't start with that!"

He asked again. "Well, help me to make sense out that."

She cut him off curtly. "I don't want to talk about it."

Her tone suggested he had no right to even ask her the question.

That triggered in him the emotion that must have been smoldering just under the surface of his consciousness.

His curiosity turned to indignation. Of course he had a right to ask. He had every right to ask. She had made a commitment to him. He had made it perfectly clear to her, two years earlier, that he was not going to pour himself into helping Sean without her changing. Changing included, obviously, not drinking with their alcoholic son. And, how could she not expect to be held accountable for such behavior?

This was no longer a quiet discussion. It was heated. She responded, "Well, I wasn't going to give up **my drinking!**" The defensive resentment echoed off the windshield.

He retorted that, indeed, when it came to Sean, it was expected she would have given up her drinking.

She then begged off, claiming that now was not the time to bring up or discuss this.

Mentally, he acknowledged her to be correct. But his past experience told him she would NEVER be willing to address the question.

At the same moment, Maria-Teresa spoke up loudly in Louella's defense. She took up her mother's plea this was not the appropriate time.

Your Grandfather made it clear to his daughter that she did not have the knowledge or the place to speak up and this matter was not hers.

Nonetheless, he became silent. It was not the time. The exchange of less than five minutes had filled the vehicle with tension. He had become enraged and realized it. He also knew no good would come from any other words being spoken.

He reviewed the exchange, his emotions, and the events that led to the question. He was now certain – 100% certain – she had betrayed them. She had betrayed him and she had betrayed Sean.

Even as he realized this, he became angry at himself. How naïve he had been. How could he have, once again, made assumptions that she had changed? How could he have been so stupid?

He was furious. He was furious at Louella, and at himself. The anger welled up inside of him.

This bull-shit. This dysfunctional relationship. This lying. This stupidity.

DECEPTION:

Louella knew Sean resumed drinking after he came off of house arrest, the summer before. Yet, she did not face the truth of this. She did not address his behavior. She did not take a clear and firm stand for sobriety. And she did not mobilize the support system Sean had developed during the previous year.

Sean – with Louella's approval -- had deceived his Father regarding the timely return to Prescott. After his Dad had found Sean drunk -- with his cousin, Pat -- they had agreed a rapid return to the support in Prescott and away from the temptations in New Mexico was best. Louella, even if she might have had good intentions, did not get Sean to safety. Moreover, with what my friend now knew, she had tolerated and condoned --and even participated in – his resumed drinking.

Deception also surrounded the issue of fatherhood. Sean's postponing a talk with his Father about having a child should have raised red flags in the mind of a mature parent. Why wait? His Dad had poured himself out to help Sean. Repeatedly. And, over the previous three and a half years, Sean's Dad had sacrificed immensely for his son's benefit. Why should Sean wait to inform his best ally? That question should have been posed to Sean by his mother. And she should have lead Sean back to his support and guide, his friend and his father, the one she herself had turned to when Sean had most needed help.

ASSUMPTIONS AND NAIVETE:

With the new information of the past 48 hours, my friend saw his flaws too clearly. Once he got Sean settled in, at Prescott, in the summer of 2010, he should have followed through with much more involvement.

Not participating in the family conference held by the program that fall was the beginning. He should not have accepted the excuses of Sean, of Louella, and even of Maria-Teresa. Neither Louella nor Maria-Teresa had participated in any of the programs or information through the 2008 intervention. There was much for them to learn. All three should have sacrificed to get to that first fall program.

And when he and Louella did go to the family conference in the spring, he didn't push for Maria-Teresa to attend. Another slip-up on his part.

When he dropped Sean off that summer in 2010, he knew his relationship with his son needed to continue to grow. He addressed this with the therapist at the program several times. He erred in accepting the therapist's explanation that it should not be pushed. The relationship had been steadily improving while Sean was in Aspiro, and in Oregon. It was now clear "Why not continue to build it?"

Sean and the program's therapist did not go deeply enough into the mental and emotional issues and into the problems that formed the basis for Sean's self-destructive choices over the years. Only now, after the events of the past 48 hours did this failure become clear to him. Sean had failed to fully internalize change. My friend had assumed the therapist would have taken Sean into the deep psychological work he needed – the CEBT Sean was so ready for. Looking back, he came to suspect that with Sean's busy schedule in college and with his (superficial) laudatory behavior, the therapist got lulled into thinking Sean was doing better than he really was. I am not sure anyone really understands what a painful realization this has been for my friend. A crucial realization: too late.

He also wrestled with his failure to hold Louella accountable in her commitment to learn. He saw the faux pas between her and the therapist, at the spring family conference, as cause for future action, by the therapist. One of many issues he didn't follow through on.

Assumptions and naïveté. Your Grandfather had to face his own failures.

When Sean had successfully finished his first year in Prescott, and he returned to face the judge, my friend did not go with Sean to court. He failed to be there to witness and participate in Sean's praise and success.

Moreover, by not going, he had made another blunder, too. He was not there to protest to the judge that Sean should NOT take the house arrest at his mother's place, but rather at his Father's.

My friend had assumed Sean would ask the judge to stay at his Father's if house arrest was required. But by the time your Granddad was aware of the decision, a different plan had been locked into. And then he did not push hard enough to change that plan. In retrospect, this may have been the fatal lapse. For Sean was to resume drinking under Louella's watch and without his Father's awareness.

And there were even more assumptions and naïveté he faced on this drive home.

When he had found Sean drinking – loaded, with his cousin, after house arrest had ended and before the wedding – he failed to appreciate the severity or seriousness. He had not stayed close enough to Sean and he continued to have idealistic expectations of Louella.

All of this was a continuation of his pattern of assumptions and naïveté.

Your Grandfather chewed on all these things as he drove.

Ever so slowly the tension lessened. Nothing was going to bring back his son.

Yet, more and more he felt Louella's betrayal – and his failures.

This dysfunction in which Sean had been trapped since his youth was not just unfortunate...

Chapter 32 -- IT DIDN'T HAVE TO HAPPEN

It was tragic.

It was the major cause of Sean's premature death.

What happened up on those rocks?

What were the mistakes Sean made?

Sean had not properly assessed the face of the rock. It had ledges. It was not smooth. Moreover, it angled in such a way that any fall would not be a freefall. A fall would be on to, and not free from, the hard surface.

Sean had not appreciated the quality of the rock. It could not accept -- or hold -- the "piece" he planned to place, at least not where he placed it.

Sean had carelessly chosen to go up far beyond the protection of the belay.

Sean had not chosen someone with more experience than his to belay him. Cody deferred to Sean, who apparently had more experience. Cody was not prepared to shout out insecurity to Sean.

Sean had chosen not to wear his helmet.

And Sean had been using marijuana and drinking alcohol[6] -
- Sean chose to drink alcohol and then climb.

Your Grandfather was certain. Sean's death was not an
accident[7].

Sean died because of a series of mistakes.

Why?

Why did he make those mistakes?

Some would say it was because he was young.

Some would say rock climbing is about risk-taking.

Some will insist it was an accident.

---

[6] Jordan, a co-climber that day (but not with Sean at the time of the fall)
could not deny Sean was drinking. He acknowledged that some of the
climbers had been drinking beer at lunch before heading out to Granite
Dells. And he stated "I don't think he'd drink a lot with rock
climbing." Kevin Keith, the firefighter and first responder who was up
on the rocks ministering to Sean as he died, told your Grandfather that
he smelled alcohol. And, eventually, the toxicology report from the
Medical Examiner's Office proved what was already obvious: the
presence in Sean's body of ethyl alcohol and THC
(tetrahydrocannabinol).
[7] If one goes barreling down the highway, on four new tires, properly
mounted and inflated, and has a blowout, the outcome is an accident. If
one goes barreling down the highway, on four bald tires, out of
alignment and improperly inflated, and has a blowout, the outcome is
not an accident.

My friend could not.

He knew better.

He knew Sean made those mistakes due to, in large part, the failures of his parents.

Your Granddad knew some people might tell him he was just speculating. Or, that he was feeling guilty. Or, maybe someone would claim this kind of thinking can happen sometimes in a parent when they lose a child too young.

And he knew he could never prove, to the satisfaction of many, what he realized. But your Grandfather Michael, my friend, was certain your Dad didn't have to die.

His reasoning went like this.

At this time in history and in this country, the most common cause of premature death in youth is accidents. And accidental death in adolescents is more common in males than in females. Young men often think and act as if they are indestructible.

In Sean's case, when you add his ADD, it is as if he were an adolescent male "on steroids." Such a person was even more likely to take risks.

Over the years, Sean had refused to learn how to live with ADD. To Sean, ADD was another label; another badge of dishonor. While he might, at times, have accepted that he had ADD, he preferred to NOT deal with it. Because of his disunited parents, when it came to ADD an atmosphere of acceptance, support, order, and encouragement was never created, the type of atmosphere in which he could grow.

The ADD was never effectively addressed. As a result he never learned the skills that can compensate for the impulsivity of ADD.

In addition to ADD, there was alcoholism – and, there too, the family dysfunction kept them all from dealing properly with alcoholism.

Sean's alcohol intake that day certainly played a role in his mistakes. No one will ever know for sure how much. But all the statistics about drunken driving show that judgment and coordination are impaired under the influence of alcohol. Drinking and rock climbing are just as foolish a combination.

His mother had taught Sean it was OK to resume drinking. And his father was not involved enough to be aware he had resumed drinking.

But it wasn't just alcohol on the day of his death. It was also, and probably more importantly, the indirect effects of alcoholism – over many years -- that was a major factor in his death. The family's failure – Sean's, Louella's, and his Father's -- to effectively deal with alcoholism caused a long series of decisions over many years that culminated in Sean being who he was and how he approached life. Day after day, year after year, Sean chose to --and was allowed to -- spend time seeking out and experiencing alcohol and drugs. And each day spent in that manner was a day not spent growing in wisdom, knowledge, and experience.

The alcoholism within the family stunted his maturation and thwarted the process of his becoming an adult.

Chronologically, Sean was 27 years old. But Sean was not 27 years mature. Given the arrested development associated with his addiction, it is reasonable to estimate that Sean had caught up, as a result of the intensive interventions, to his early 20's -- psychologically, emotionally, and mentally -- by the time of his death. But he was not 27 years mature on the day of his death.

During adolescence a young man should experience controlled risk, under the tutelage, guidance, and direction of mature adults – including and particularly parents. Sean did not have such experiences. During his adolescence, Sean was living an undisciplined and unstructured life; and he had been taught disrespect of his father and of authority. Even though he was 27 years old in body, he had not had the experiences he could have and should have had by that age.[8]

Sean could have and should have had such opportunities and experiences.

---

[8] A simple application of this reasoning follows: No Boy Scout who had reached the level of Eagle Scout would have made such a series of mistakes. In order to reach Eagle status a young man must, among other things, earn a sizeable number of Merit Badges. Each badge requires about 20-25 hours of work, some more, some less. In the process of earning each the young man must (a) stay focused on the task or issue until the badge is earned (tenacity), (b) give up other activities or choices to accomplish the task at hand (delay or substitute gratification), and (c) work with others who are more knowledgeable (learn his limitations and experience humility). Such a process, done repeatedly, teaches many things, among them caution and appropriate consideration of risk.

Your Grandfather was certain that no Eagle Scout would have ever put himself in such a dangerous position as Sean did.

My friend had example after example that told him his son had been cheated. Over and over Sean's Father had witnessed patients with diseases and illnesses that could easily have killed. However, with united, effective, and loving support and sacrifice from others – primarily family – great odds had been overcome, and life was prolonged. Sean did not have such a family system united in loving support and sacrifice on his behalf.

Sean's parents had failed him.

Mariah, your Dad didn't have to die -- up there on those rocks as he did.

SECTION II -- MISTAKES, WHAT-IFS, AND OTHER LESSONS

LESSONS 1 -- THE DANGER OF DIVIDED PARENTING

Mariah, in the story, we described the conflict between your Grandfather and Louella.

By now you should know, from the story that it didn't have to be that way. Your Dad did not have to be trapped between them in the way he was.

When Sean was enrolled in the first wilderness program, Second Nature, they provided teaching that could and should have ended the parental conflict and set Sean's life onto a stable, positive path. That program had extensive educational material available to the parents of those enrolled. Your Granddad read as much as he could. Louella refused to participate, if you remember the story.

My friend was delighted when he came across, in their educational materials, descriptions of the negative interpersonal dynamics within the family. He tried hard to share this information with Louella. He copied information and gave it to her. It broke his heart she refused.

Don't you ever refuse to learn! Don't you ever refuse to help those that you love!

Here, some of that material is shared in more detail.

ON PARENTING STYLES
Your Granddad's natural Parenting Style was
"Authoritative."

Louella's Parenting Style was "Permissive."

When Louella became "Permissive", Sean's Dad would
occasionally revert from "Authoritative" to an
"Authoritarian" Parenting Style.

Here is what they taught; you will see the wedge of
constant pressure Sean experienced:

> ### The explanation:
> *Parenting style refers to how a parent encourages,*
> *challenges, and teaches a child to complete tasks*
> *and exhibit appropriate behavior. Family*
> *researchers have identified four different parenting*
> *styles. Although no parent will completely fit into*
> *just one style all the time, many parents will often*
> *gravitate towards a style that achieves the desired*
> *results. Most of us jump in and out of these styles*
> *frequently depending on several emotional factors.*
> *The following explanations will include a simple*
> *example about incomplete homework to help*
> *demonstrate.*

Here is your Grandfather Michael's preferred or natural
style. It is also the one he grew up with:

> ### Authoritative Parenting Style
> *The authoritative parenting style is characterized by*
> *consistently setting and enforcing rules and limits*
> *while doing so in an assertive, clear, and thoughtful*

manner. This style differs from the "Authoritarian style" because there is an effort to balance power and compassion. Authoritative parents often discuss rules and consequences (both positive and negative) as a way of creating awareness and teaching both short and long-term accountability. Rules and consequences are enforced because they teach important lessons about responsibility in relationships and society's norms. Parents who use this style don't feel the same need to push or lecture as other parents because they are allowing the child to make reasonable mistakes and to learn from the consequences of those mistakes. When the experience is teaching the child, the parent is able to guide and support with love and empathy.

Authoritative parents often have some awareness of how their emotions and beliefs influence their children. These parents are less likely to transfer or project their issues on to those around them. Ideally, they can articulate requests and feelings with some clarity and resist the instinct to let their emotions decide the punishments. They don't try to use guilt, fear, or other forms of manipulation to change their child's behavior. They respond to their child's emotions, thoughts, and behaviors, instead of focusing exclusively on performance. These parent are still enforcing boundaries but can also be found taking time to sit, discuss, and assess their child's issues before consequences are enforced. In the example of homework, these parents are asking questions and considering both internal and external factors, such as the opposite sex, drugs use, learning disabilities, emotional stress, or other factors to identify possible reasons for incomplete work. Once issues are identified, they respond to the problem by joining or aligning themselves with the child to deal with the issue.

Here Louella's style is described (with some emphasis added by me in the form of underlining):

Permissive Parenting Style

The permissive parenting style may encourage individuality and creativity, but does not provide effective structure and boundaries for the child's behavior. Similar to other parents, they are overwhelmed and intimidated by new challenges in parenting. They may feel uncertain when to say 'yes' and 'no'. In this style, parents may be compensating for their own childhood experiences or an authoritarian parent. It is not uncommon for one parent to move more toward the authoritarian while the other moves toward the permissive parenting style. At times, these styles may become extreme, as each attempt to compensate for what he/she sees as the flawed parenting style of the other parent. This "polarization" of parents is particularly prevalent in divorced parents. <u>Children will often pull towards the more permissive parent in order to manipulate a situation so they get what they want</u> as well as for emotional safety. Because parents are constantly dealing with their own relationships, professional challenges, and social lives, they become overwhelmed and fail to provide structure, rules and consequences for their child's developmental needs.

Some permissive parents are afraid of their child's opinion of them and attempt to gain their approval by indulging the child or permitting behavior that normally would lead to natural or logical consequences. This pattern of parenting is often found in divorce or adoption situations. These parents passively support inappropriate behavior because they feel guilt or some responsibility for their child's situation. Parents that use this style sometimes rationalize destructive behavior or reward their child when they have not earned it. _This parenting style often looks like "a lot of fun"_ to the neighbor _children and parents feel temporarily more involved or accepted_ by the child. _Co-dependence in both parent and child are often found_ in these homes and _the relationship is often called enmeshed or enabling_. When dealing with the homework example, these parents are much more involved. Permissive parents often micro-manage academic progress. They will go way out of their way to create success for their child. Sometimes, these parents are found over-celebrating minors achievements, doing projects or assignments for their child, bending deadlines, or creating excuses to prevent their child from dealing with failure.

Children of permissive parents are egocentric and have a hard time being told 'no' by other authority figures or in relationships. _They often crave attention and structure from parents, but don't want to experience the delay of gratification necessary to develop discipline. These children notice when the permissive parent attempts to enforce limits or consequences and usually manipulates the parent until the permissive style returns._ They are aware that their parent is intimidated by the idea of confrontation. They sense that the parent feels responsible for the child's mood and they use it to their advantage. Some parents go back and forth

between permissive and authoritarian parenting
styles, depending on the situation.

And here is the Authoritarian Style your Grandfather would
sometimes revert to, when he found Louella too permissive.
Once he learned this information, he was able to
consciously do his best to keep from slipping into this style.

Authoritarian Parenting Style
The authoritarian style is sometimes referred to as
"drill sergeant" parenting. This parent puts an
emphasis on compliance, strict rules, specific
expectations, and performance. The goals of this
style usually focus on supervising, teaching, and
protecting the child. A 'drill sergeant' parent is
typically found lecturing, threatening, and arguing
with their child. Similar to the distant parenting
style, they use the child's feelings of guilt, shame,
and embarrassment to elicit behavioral change. The
underlying message communicated by this style is
"You have proven your incompetence by your
decisions and you should no longer have the
freedom to act on your own. I will take control and
make decisions and consequences for you."

Although these parents love their child, their child
usually experiences them as emotionally distant,
irritable, angry, or performance oriented. Because
this style focuses on getting the child to show
specific behaviors, children often fear this parent
and create lies or put on an emotional mask to
temporarily satisfy parental expectations. For
example: These parents will lecture and threaten
disciplinary action if high grades are not achieved.
They will guilt or attempt to scare their child with
the ideas of future failure and will connect all future

*happiness or worth to high performance.
Unfortunately, if they are found spending time with
their child working on homework, they are
impatient and are pointing out flaws and
underachievement. They often see emotional issues,
social distress, and learning difficulties as excuses
and avoidant behavior and strict rules and
punishment are the only answer.*

*Although the authoritarian parenting style may
motivate children in the short term, it hinders an
individual's ability to problem solve and learn
valuable lessons in relationships. Unfortunately,
sensitive children feel weak around this parent and
eventually develop resentment for this style. These
children will often try to find ways to prove his/her
strength by exacting revenge or rebelling against
the parent's beliefs. They might also try to create
stronger personalities outside the home. Another
consequence of this style is that children become
excessively submissive and unable to stand up to
peer pressure. They also tend to try and avoid any
conflict in relationships. They end up believing that
they are weak and often become dependent on
praise from peers or significant relationships.*

It was regrettable that Louella had not taken the
opportunity to learn these simple things when Sean was in
Second Nature. Sean's Dad took the time to print out this
material and send it to her, but she never responded. She
never changed. As a result, Sean never experienced the
consistent structure and boundaries of healthy parenting
from a united team.

From the time he was little, Sean had been, understandably,
attracted to his mother's permissive parenting style. Any

child would have been. And, true to the researchers experiences described above, he became a master of manipulation. (See the underlined areas above.)

In addition, because of his parents' failure to unite in his parenting, Sean's inability to delay gratification (also described and underlined above) could never be successfully tempered with proper guidance. It is certain that lack of guidance played into his risk-taking behavior, as described in the story. It is reasonable to presume it played a role in his decisions on the day he died.

THE DRAMA TRIANGLE

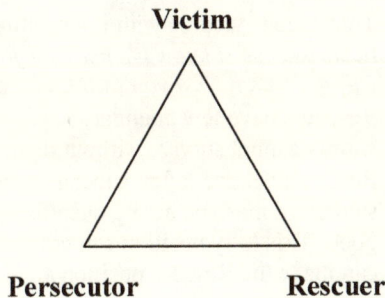

In another section of the educational material was described a pattern of interaction called the "Drama Triangle."

When your Grandfather read this, he could see that dynamic within the family.

Here is that description:

Drama Triangle

Victim

Persecutor   **Rescuer**

ROLES:

Victim
- Takes no responsibilities for actions or feelings
- They discount their capabilities: "There is nothing I can do" "I am not strong enough" "Everyone is against me"
- Places the majority of responsibility of success and failure onto others
- Complains about all the reasons why something cannot be done. Often plays the "yes-but" game.
- When you suggest a change, they will say yes that is a good idea, but it won't work for me.
- Predominant feelings - helplessness and hopelessness
- Pathetic Victim - "Poor me" "I don't know how this happened"
- Angry Victim - Pretends to be powerful, yet at same time denying responsibility "look what you've done to me"
- Victims use blame and guilt to manipulate others into doing what they want.
- Victims hook up with people they can blame for their sorry state of affairs.

Rescuer
- Rescuers discount the ability of others to solve their own problems
- They are the proverbial knights in shining armor, selflessly putting their needs aside to come to the aid of others
- They "feed" victims with information they want to hear, such as *"I know it's not your fault"* or *"Things will get better, just you wait and see"*
- Rescuers have few boundaries, presuming that others simply cannot survive without them
- Rescuers believe, often subconsciously, that they are saints and martyrs, acting unselfishly for other's good. This lofty position can create a "high" which can make the Rescuer position addictive and all encompassing.
- The main message they send to others is: *"You are inept. You cannot take care of yourself. You are not*

*good enough. Therefore I will be in charge. I will
take care of you"*

- They may see themselves as a rescue-martyr and then
  end up as a victim-martyr
- Separates others who have conflict rather than
  bringing them together to resolve conflicts.
- Predominant feeling-guilt

Persecutor
- Plays the "bad guy"
- Act largely out of anger and rage
- By criticizing, demeaning, and discounting others,
  the persecutor sets the other two positions in motion -
  the victim abdicates responsibility for what is wrong
  and the rescuer tries in vain to fix it.
- They maintain control by playing off of the
  helplessness of the victim or the guilt of the rescuer.
  This ploy contributes to their control, which
  generates a feeling of omnipotence not unlike the
  "high" the rescuer gets from aiding and abetting the
  victim's hopelessness.
- Persecutors will criticize others without giving
  guidance how to improve. They also tend to remind
  others of their past mistakes.
- Predominant feeling – anger

My friend could see how this dynamic, while not rigidly
adhered to, was a recurrent pattern within the family. Sean
was usually the Victim. Louella - the rescuer. Grandpa -
the Persecutor. Though, occasionally, Louella and Grandpa
would play the opposite roles.

The program's materials offered insight on ways to break
out of the dysfunction:

Getting Out of the Triangle (Key word is Empowering)
- Teaching students about the triangle - bringing the
  roles into consciousness

- Running a group on the triangle and asking students to look at times where they have played these roles
- Discussing the pros and cons of giving up the roles
- After student has understanding of roles, point out times when you see them playing the role
- Helping students be bold enough to tell the truth about their feelings and motives
- Helping students recognize that they indeed have options, choices (albeit tough ones)
- Helping explore these options without "telling them what to do" or admonishing (persecuting) them for allowing themselves to be in such a predicament in the first place
- Balancing boundaries with empathy
- Processing your experience with student in DAPS (i.e. "when you're playing the victim, this is the experience I have ... " or asking questions like "who do I remind you of right now?")

Answer the Following Questions:

1. Explain how this model relates to your family. Which role do you typically take? Which role does your child typically take? Your spouse/ex-spouse, siblings, etc.?

2. Although we each have a role we most identify with, we will also rotate through the other positions, going completely around the triangle, sometimes in a matter of minutes, or even seconds, many times every day. All roles eventually lead back to victim. In which way have you played the role of victim?

3. Whenever we assume either the persecutor or rescuer roles, we come across as superior. From either position we relate as though we are better, stronger, smarter, or more-together than the victim. Sooner or later the victim will retaliate out of resentment for feeling looked down upon in their inferior position. As a persecutor or rescuer, how may this have harmed your relationship with your son or daughter?

4.   Now that you have an understanding of the Drama
     Triangle and each role that you and your family members
     play, how can this awareness help you to not engage in
     the perpetuating cycle of the triangle in the future?

One way to seeing and saying:
- Louella adored Sean and was devoted to him, but
  through her adoration and devotion she didn't
  protect Sean -- from himself.
- Grandpa understood -- life and Sean. Grandpa was
  usually right about things. But his understanding
  and being correct didn't protect Sean either.

Sean never had the benefit of a healthy, functioning family
within which to grow and mature.   That was the basic
tragedy that led to Sean's premature death.

Mariah, you do not have to repeat this. You do not have to
live life dysfunctionally.

LESSONS 2 – OF ANGER AND APOLOGY

Mariah, in one of the chapters, I talk about "Too Much of a Good Thing."

I think it can be argued that your Granddad had too much of a good thing in "forgiveness."

This notion overlaps with his naïveté, as he came to understand.

You see, Mariah, your Grandfather had become a very angry man. The problem was: he hadn't consciously recognized that.

After Sean's death -- not too many days after -- he and his wife Cindy were reading from a morning devotional[9] -- a book written by Gary Chapman. In the reading for that day Dr. Chapman mentioned anger. He talked of anger in the context of marriage, and referenced his book "*Anger, Handling a Powerful Emotion in a Healthy Way*." At the time my friend was still very angry at all the betrayal he experienced in the days following Sean's death. That particular morning, as he reflected on the massage, your Grandfather decided to find that book. Intuitively, he sensed the book could help him.

---

[9] Titled "The One Year, Love Language Minute."

Little did he know how much that book would help him, over time.

The book came and he read. Very early in the book Dr. Chapman makes the case that anger is NOT BAD, that anger is "evidence that we are made in God's image."

Reading those words and realizing what they meant were like opening up a sealed vault (unconscious) inside of my friend.

He had repeatedly been told that God wanted us to forgive.

Over and over: "Forgiveness."

The words of the "Lord's Prayer" had been chiseled into his mind: "Forgive us our trespasses as we forgive those who trespass against us."

Dr. Chapman went on to explain a modification of this teaching. He reasons that God experiences anger[10]. To paraphrase: as a loving Parent, God wants His sons and daughters to be good (sinless). As a loving parent he is angry when they disobey (sin). Like any loving parent, He knows the detrimental effects of disobedience (sin) and wants to protect His children from harm (negative consequences). Thus, anger is His logical -- and loving -- response to sin (injustice or unrighteousness).

---

[10] He points out that the word "anger" is found 455 times in the Old Testament; 375 times referring to God's anger. He points out in the Gospels where Jesus exhibits His anger.

His reasoning continues: We are made in God's image. That is why we experience anger when we witness or experience injustice (sin; being wronged).[11]

Dr. Chapman argues that it is not only OK, but it is right to feel angry in the face of sin (being wronged, injustice).

Once my friend understood and grasped the logic and goodness in Dr. Chapman's insight, it freed him to experience (rather than suppress) his anger.

As your Grandfather read on in the book and reflected on his life, he saw the pattern. And he came to see a paradoxical destructiveness in the repeated swallowing or suppressing of just anger.[12]

My friend had made a habit of pushing himself to forgive others who acted unjustly toward him. When he read the book and carried out one of Dr. Chapman's recommended exercises, he found a very long list of people who had hurt him unjustly. The list went back to when he was a young child.

Trying to be a good person, as he had come to understand what that meant, your Grandfather had repeatedly done his best to forgive everyone. He now recognized the mistake in this.

A righteous anger should not be swallowed, and forgiveness should not be given automatically. An anger

---

[11] He is careful to distinguish a righteous anger from anger that is not rooted in or the result of injustice. The book is worth reading.
[12] The destructiveness probably played a role – albeit indirectly --in Sean's life experiences, and in his premature death.

that wells up inside from being treated unjustly begs to be examined and considered.

It is possible, after reflection, one may conclude that the best way to deal with a specific anger is to forgive. However, on the other hand – and equally out of love -- the best way to deal with anger may be to confront the injustice and seek to right the wrong.

My friend became conscious of an unhealthy pattern in his life. Far too often, he had inappropriately swallowed anger that begged to be faced. Some of the injustices behind his anger should not have been readily forgiven but rather courageously confronted. As a result of his practice of attempting universal forgiveness he had failed to develop the capacity, strength, and skill to face injustice firmly and lovingly.

As part of his misunderstanding, he had assumed, far too often, that the one who had wronged him would, as he did, reflect on behavior, recognize error[13], and "self-correct."

This pattern marked his relationships with Louella and with Sean. The result: wrongs were repeated, to the detriment of those he loved.

By failing to appreciate the potential goodness that can come from anger, he had allowed evil to insinuate itself into his life – tragically.

---

[13] Allow one's conscience to tell oneself what is right or wrong.

Mariah, you might benefit by reviewing the story; Sean and your Granddad's story. Look at the times your Grandfather was treated unfairly, wrongly, or unjustly. You will see that frequently he did not directly address the mistreatment.

If he had, would not events have unfolded differently?

And what of apology?

Apology is a wonderful, albeit imperfect, antidote for resentment. Most of us, most of the time, will feel differently about any injustice we have received -- real or perceived -- if the perpetrator apologizes.

Gary Chapman [again, Dr. Chapman!!], together with a fellow author, has another book, this one on apology.[14] Mariah, it is worthwhile to read and think about what he says in this book, too.

Some people sense that apologizing is an indication of inferiority or weakness. To apologize, they feel, makes one vulnerable. In reality, apologizing is NOT a sign of fragility or powerlessness. Rather it is a sign of strength and self-confidence. Someone who is self-confident, thoughtful, considerate, and kind can and will apologize when he realizes he has made a mistake that hurts another. Those who are uncertain, unthinking, insensitive, or selfish are not likely to apologize.

Apologies are the means of mending and healing damaged relationships.

---

[14] *The Five Languages of Apology*, by Gary Chapman and Jennifer Thomas.

We are all not only capable of injuring others; we are virtually assured of doing so by our very nature. Without apology the injured party is left to wonder if the one behind the wrong is going to repeat the behavior; or if she is even aware that she is responsible for the hurtful consequences thereof.

What of those who are not aware that they have wronged another?

None of us is going to apologize if we are not aware we have harmed or hurt someone[15]. Thus, we see one of the reasons to respond to being unjustly treated, rather than to simply accept and swallow being wronged.

We have both a need and a responsibility to share with others when we experience being hurt by them.

How would Sean's life have been different if a practice of humble apology had existed in his family?

Anger and apology: two essentials that should be understood if one is to share satisfying relationships with others.

---

[15] See the chapter on "Possible Explanations."

LESSONS 3 -- TOO MUCH OF A GOOD THING – ONE OF THE LESSONS

Mariah, this short chapter magnifies one of the lessons from the story. This chapter tries to show you how hard it can be to see the danger or evil that is right in front of you, sometimes disguised as a good thing.

"Granddad is hard working."

"Louella is charming."

"Sean is adventurous."

Too much of a good thing => is no longer a good thing.

"Granddad is hard working."

THE POSITIVES (that might be associated with this characteristic)
> Productive
> Good provider
> Work ethic
> Good employee
> Achiever

Dependable
Likely to follow through

THE NEGATIVES (that might be associated with
an excess of this characteristic)
No time for friends
No time for family
Needs to learn to play
Needs to delegate better
More balance in life is needed
Never satisfied (that work is done)
"All work and no play makes _____ (in
this case: 'your Granddad') a dull 'boy.'"
Workaholic

"Louella is charming."

THE POSITIVES (that might be associated with
this characteristic)
Fun to be around
Flattering
Good conversationalist
Enchanting
Delightful
Inspirational
Demure
Deferential
Captivating
Darling

THE NEGATIVES (that might be associated with
an excess of this characteristic)

Beguiling
Bewitching
Superficial
Tricky
Dishonest
Spell binding
Irritating
Self-centered
"Snake with forked tongue"

"Sean is adventurous."

THE POSITIVES (that might be associated with this characteristic)
Brave
Audacious
Bold
Fearless
Confident
Daring
Spunky
Exuberant
Vigorous

THE NEGATIVES (that might be associated with an excess of this characteristic)
Dangerous
Adrenaline junkie
Risk taker
At risk for: increased hospital bills
Brash
Fearless
Overconfident
Reckless

Impetuous

Your Grandfather was hard-working, somewhat
introverted, and very thoughtful.

Louella was charming, an extrovert, not so thoughtful.

When conflict arouse in the marriage, each parent's way of
being, one could say, was threatened by the other's way of
being. Each became defensive. As described, and
crucially important, effective communication and shared
introspection could not be found.

Each retreated to their own personality strengths (THE
POSITIVES, above listed).
Each failed to appreciate their own weaknesses (THE
NEGATIVES, listed above).

The differences between the two became exaggerated. The
negatives went unchecked. Indeed, the negatives became
amplified.

Your Dad got squeezed between the two polarizing
opposites. In this progression, the negative aspects of
Sean's personality were never clearly identified for him and
to him. Thus, he did not, and could not, consciously
appreciate the danger to himself of "too much of a good
thing."

Stated differently (and once again), consciously or not, his
parents failed him. That failure was a major underlying

"mistake" that led to the fatal decisions Sean made on the day of his death.

Now that this is seen more clearly, you can appreciate what might seem to many people to have been merely an accidental death was really a tragic mistake that could have been averted.

Seeing all of this clearly is immensely painful. For to do so, one can see, in retrospect, how changes made before that day could have led to a series of decisions by Sean which would have markedly and drastically decreased the likelihood of a fatal fall and death.

Not seeing these things clearly is a great deal less painful than seeing these things and facing them. Unfortunately, to miss one's dark side is to miss the opportunity to grow and to change. To miss one's dark side may also deprive others. Those "others" may be the ones we care most about.

Mariah, may God give you wisdom, knowledge, and understanding – gifts of the Holy Spirit.

LESSONS 4 -- SPIRITUALLY: THE OTHER WAY TO SEE IT ALL

Your Grandfather was not very assertive when it came to spirituality. He sensed people, at least in the US, were surrounded by religions and religious messages. He thought that most people had some religion or spiritual tradition growing up. With the experiences of adult life, he came to realize this assumption was just that, another assumption on his part. As many as 92% of Americans believe in God. But how many translate that into goodness, morality, or a spiritual way of being?

He tried to be a good person. But, in reality, he didn't do a very good job. If he had, many things would have been different for Sean.

The same thing can be said about others in Sean's life. If others had been better Christians -- and virtually all claimed to be Christian, if not Catholics – it is possible Sean's soul might well have been nurtured enough to have successfully led him to make other choices than he did.

Here are some very specific examples and instances where my friend confessed his sinfulness to me.

Before they dated, he should not have condoned and participated in life denying actions of Louella and others. The Evil One had already insinuated Himself into their lives. Evil was not faced with fortitude and fear of God, but with cowardice and compromise.

271

He should not have given up his habit of morning prayers back when Sean was conceived.

He should have insisted on respect from his son (teaching him how to live the 4th commandment).

He should have taken leadership in demanding honesty within the family, complete honesty.

He should not have allowed the family to divide. "A house divided cannot stand." This may sound trite, but it was another central truth in Sean's life.

He should have blessed Sean more often.

He should have taught, more personally, an appreciation of the reality of the loving Father, an appreciation that Christ taught. An example: He should have made time, every evening, after moving back to New Mexico, from Phoenix, to pray with his two children. He had initiated this in Phoenix. He failed to continue this practice in New Mexico.

He should have insisted on Sean attending Mass -- every Sunday, at least -- when living with him. He should have been willing to put up with and deal with Sean's resistance and complaints.

He should have encouraged / insisted Sean prepare for and receive the Sacrament of Confirmation. Going through the learning and preparation for the Sacrament of Confirmation may have added to a different life.

He should have made attendance at Sacred Heart Catholic Church, just one block from his residence while in Oregon, mandatory for Sean if he was to get continued support from his Dad.

He should have made attendance at (another) Sacred Heart Catholic Church, just two blocks from his college in Prescott, mandatory for Sean if he was to get continued support from his Dad.

Throughout Sean's life, he should have shared his values and beliefs more freely and openly.

He should have been the spiritual leader in the household.

Although he prayed a great deal during most of the periods of his life, my friend came to the sense maybe he should have trusted in and relied on God, more than on himself, in dealing with relationships and issues.

It would be easy to suggest or to point out apparent spiritual lapses and failures of others. Such judgment is best left to a Higher Power.

However, you, Mariah, are advised to develop a keen conscience as part of your spiritual life. Having your Interior Guide always available to you can save much suffering. Saving you from suffering is the very reason your Loving Father urges and challenges you to daily examine your choices and to constantly strive to become closer to Him and to Goodness.

During the long drive back from Prescott two days after Sean's death, when he prayed, my friend shared that he had the sense that God told him "Don't be mad at Me, I have done you a favor."

He came back to and reflected upon that comment, many times. It was the only message he discerned in his repeated praying, about Sean and his death.

He sensed that God was telling him that He had saved your Grandfather from witnessing Sean's ongoing suffering, for years into the future. It was clear from what he learned those two days in Prescott that Sean's struggle and suffering were not at all over as he had thought. Sean had resumed drinking. His mother had resumed her enabling -- and worse. Sean, at the time of his death, was still very much caught in the pincers of conflict: internal and external.

My friend had made it clear, when he answered Louella's plea to help Sean, that he would not rescue Sean ever again. What would Sean have done, and what would my friend have had to witness, with the next crisis caused by drinking? Based on the past, it was likely to be just a matter of time before the drinking once again caused dangerous behavior[16].

_____

[16] Indeed, hadn't it already? Isn't that what led to Sean's death?

LESSONS 5 -- MISTAKES

A Wise Man Learns from the Mistakes of Others.
The Average Man Learns from His Own Mistakes.
The Fool Fails to Learn.

Here is a list of some mistakes. The astute reader will have found others.

<u>SEAN</u>

Immediate/ at the end
- Climbing without a helmet
- Climbing too high above last secure anchor bolt in the rock
- Failing to appreciate the danger inherent in the ledges/irregular face of the rock, should he fall
- Placing undue reliance on an inexperienced belayer
- Over-estimating his abilities (failing to be humble, lacking humility)
- Allowing alcohol to be involved

Intermediate/ near the end
- Resumption of drinking after summer 2011
- Accepting drinking by others close to him and/or allowing himself to associate with drinkers
- Refusing to see and guard against his mother's role in his alcoholism

Long-term/ on-going

- Refusing treatment for ADD
- Refusing to learn about non-pharmacologic treatment of ADD
- Failing to "Honor" his father (4th Commandment)
- Being seduced into the "easier path" by others, including his mother

GRANDDAD

Specific and/or near the end
- Failure to insist on Sean's taking "house arrest" at his home, rather than Louella's
- Failure to stay closer in touch with Sean once he settled in Prescott
- Failure to recognize the severity of Sean's relapse into alcohol the summer before his death
- Failure to appreciate the profound risks of relapse
- Failure to protect (even attempt to seriously protect) Sean from those who misled him
- Failure to appreciate what he (Granddad) could do (more) to help Sean in his maturation process, a process crucial to Sean's development of self-esteem, self-discipline, and humility

General, long-term, and/or on-going
- Failure to evidence love (blessing) of Sean, primarily and unconditionally
- Failure to be spiritual leader in household
- Failure to hold Louella justly accountable to truth, from onset of relationship with her
- Failure to be an example of manly strength for Sean
- Failure to protect Maria-Teresa from negative effects of Sean's choices, and better model for her behavior that could, in turn, have helped Sean

- Failure to make more time for Sean, and for their relationship

LOUELLA

<u>Near the End</u>
- Allowing Sean to resume drinking at end of summer of 2011, after the end of house arrest:
- Not protecting Sean from those who would allow -- or would encourage -- his resumption of drinking at that time.
- Not removing Sean from temptations that caused him to resume drinking, at that time, by returning him to the treatment program and the sober support network in Prescott.
- Not notifying Sean's Dad and/or the Prescott treatment program, and thereby mobilizing intervention and support for Sean (and herself), when Sean resumed and continued his dangerous drinking, from summer of 2011 to his death.
- Actually joining with Sean in drinking alcohol, sending the loudest possible message of "no support" to an alcoholic.

<u>Along the Way</u>
- After Sean's first DWI, paying off his loan for him rather than support him in his responsibility to fully accept the consequences of his behavior (having to hire and pay a lawyer; thus the need for the loan).
- Refusing to honor her commitment (and her responsibility as a mother) to come back to New Mexico, from Phoenix, and work with Sean's Dad to address Sean's alcohol and drug use when this problem became fully apparent late in his high school years.

- Supporting Sean's irresponsible behavior, for four years, from the time he flunked out of New Mexico State University until the first wilderness intervention.
- Getting her alcoholic son a job at a bar.
- Refusing to participate in Sean's care through the first wilderness program, and thereby denying him the unified support he needed; while simultaneously refusing to learn about her role in his problem.
- Removing Sean from the treatment program in Washington State (Straight Arrow), by lying to the program directors; and simultaneously teaching Sean to lie and to manipulate others through lying.
- Not just allowing her alcoholic son to drink but taking him with her to functions where both would drink, which fed his ongoing irresponsibility and eventually led to additional DWI's.
- Not keeping her commitment to Granddad which she made in order to garner his help for Sean in the winter of 2009-10. This included failure to learn about and change her role in his illness. (Or was this just a manipulative lie from the moment the commitment was made?)
- Ultimately, failing to accept not only her enabling and codependency, but also her own alcoholism.

At the Beginning
- Not fully accepting Sean's dyslexia to the level of educating her family about the issue and mobilizing their support for Sean and his heroic efforts and sacrifice which would have resulted in a united and very positive message to Sean, and a positive self-image within him.
- Not creating the structured environment required for someone with ADD within which can be

experienced the ability to live within boundaries and thrive despite the impulsivity of the disorder.

****

Until Sean's death my friend had bit his tongue hard, when it came to Louella and Sean.

He saw her, for years, in a position to have helped Sean. She could have minimized Sean's suffering for so many years. And she could have, at least, allowed Sean to mature in a healthy and normal manner even if she could not have raised him herself in this manner. If Sean had been allowed a healthy maturation, as is laid out in the story, Sean would not have taken the multiple risks he did on the day of his death.

Some may criticize my friend for sharing this belief of his. Yet, when all is considered -- all that Louella did, or did not do -- it is hard to understand how anyone could be so deceitful and could have refused to face truth by keeping it locked up inside. It can now be argued your Granddad's error is not that he is now addressing and sharing these insights. Rather, his error was in not addressing the sins and evils sooner (see the chapters on *Spirituality* and *Anger*) – before Sean's death. It is unfortunate and tragic that my friend did not find a successful way – in time to protect his son. (Again, consider the chapter on *Anger*.)

****

<u>GRANDDAD'S RELATIVES (different ones in different ways) and LOUELLA'S RELATIVES (different ones in different ways)</u>

- Being unwilling to accept the labels (the diagnoses) of dyslexia, ADD, and/or alcoholism. Thus forcing Sean to live a conflicted life[17].
- Not being open to new information regarding dyslexia, and thereby being unwilling or unable to support Sean's heroic effort to live successfully with dyslexia. As a result Sean missed out on the affirmation needed to develop self-esteem.
- Being unwilling to learn about Attention Deficit Disorder. Thus, being unable to positively support Sean in developing the skills needed to live productively and safely with this affliction.
- Allowing Sean to drink in their presence, even after his alcoholism was well established as a major illness and a significant problem for him.
- Drinking with Sean; i.e. condoning and sharing in Sean's wrongful, self-defeating, and destructive behavior.
- Encouraging Sean to drink; being a fully active participant is his problem and a temptation to him.
- Misleading Sean into believing that his problems, including the alcoholism, were "no big deal." And thereby subverting his efforts to develop the self-discipline needed to choose rightly.

---

[17] He lived each day with the reality of each diagnosis (the very symptoms and signs of each were part of his life). Yet the rejection, by many family and friends, of Sean's having one or more of these problems forced him to deny (or crave to deny) the reality he experienced. He was not old enough or developmentally strong enough to face older or cherished family members and friends with the realities that he faced. (See the chapter on "Possible Explanations" -- when caught with conflict between facts and feelings, the feelings usually win out.) Sean felt forced to live as if he did not have what he knew that he had. It is no wonder he was troubled for so long!

TREATMENT PROGRAMS (and Educational Consultants)

Specific
1. Second Nature (1st wilderness program)
   - Didn't pressure Louella into participation in the program and family learning
   - Didn't clearly address – to Sean – the dangerous family triangle he was in

2. Straight Arrow (organic farm in Washington State)
   - Didn't offer therapy as part of their program
   - Didn't heed warnings from Sean's Dad and from Sean's records regarding Louella's role in Sean's illness
   - Didn't involve Sean's Dad in the crucial decision to allow Louella to visit
   - Didn't involve Sean's Dad in the crucial decision to allow Louella to take Sean from the program
   - Didn't hold Louella or Sean accountable for their commitment to return Sean to the program

3. Aspiro (2nd wilderness program)
   - ?? (Hard to fault them in specifics. See "General" below.)

4. Dragonfly (Oregon)
   - Failure to individualize Sean's care as promised.
   - Failure to vigorously support Sean in his efforts to find work.
   - Failure to support Sean's interest and efforts with CEBT.

- Failure to vigorously support Sean in his efforts to resume formal education.
- Failure to monitor Sean closely.
- Failure to take Sean's inappropriate relationship with the female enrollee as a teaching/learning opportunity.
- Failing to work effectively with each of Sean's parents: Granddad in his needs and frustrations; Louella in her denial and long term role as enabler.

5. Clean Adventures
   - Didn't succeed in helping Sean to distinguish dangerous from safe relationships.
   - Didn't honor commitment to take Sean's mother back through her sequence (at family weekend), to the point of commitment from her, or (if unsuccessful) adequately warn Sean (and his Father) of the danger therein.
   - Dangerously relied on the possibility, in some nebulous future, Sean would develop the positive relationship he needed with his father; perilously assuming such could be delayed.
   - (Possibly, if aware) didn't notify my friend of Sean's resumption of dangerous drinking, after summer of 2011.

General
- Failing to adequately, clearly, and effectively describe to Sean the pathology of the family he was trapped in.

- Focusing on the "identified patient" (Sean) and not treating effectively the "real patient" which was the family and its (systemic) illness.
- And, thereby, failing to force/ demand/ expect/ arrange for adequate participation of each family member in the therapeutic program/treatment/process.

SEAN'S FELLOW CLIMBERS AND/OR FRIENDS

- Not holding one another to safety standards, the most obvious being the wearing of helmets.
- Allowing alcohol to be involved on the day of climbing, thereby increasing the risk of poor judgment.
- Putting pleasure before safety.
- (Some) chose to drink with Sean, knowing he suffered from alcoholism. Is that being a friend?

PRESCOTT COLLEGE PERSONEL

- Failure to adequately emphasize the importance of safety when climbing.
- Failure to adequately emphasize the importance of underestimating one's abilities when climbing or, to state this in reverse, the risks of overestimating one's abilities when climbing – it is crucial to have humility in the face of the force of gravity and of the unyielding hardness of rocks.

LESSONS 6 -- WHAT IF: A LIST OF "WHAT IFS"

The ability to see clearly what is right in front of us seems to be a universal challenge for humans.

Your Granddad suffered from that problem. That is, he did not always see clearly what was right in front of him.

So, too, it seems that others in Sean's life also suffered with this same defect.

The following scenarios are only conjecture. They are only guesses, if you will. Nonetheless, this exercise may help you, Mariah, to better see clearly and to understand what is right in front of you some day.

> *Indeed, those of us, when we reflect on the Passion of Our Lord, can be said to be doing this same thing.*
>
> *When one looks back at the arrest, trials, torture, condemnation, and brutal execution of an Innocent Man, isn't that part of what is considered and prayed for: to be able to see "better" in one's own life than those who condemned and crucified Jesus?*
>
> *And, the reverse, isn't that also one of the prayers: asking forgiveness for behaving in one's own life, as those who condemned, tortured, and crucified Our Lord? We ask forgiveness for those times when we failed to see clearly -- when we acted selfishly or ignorantly -- and hurt others as a consequence.*

Let us proceed with the exercise.

What if the teachers at Prescott College had seen the adventurous aspect of Sean's personality as risky for Sean? What if they knew about or saw clearly his ADD and the inherent risk a person with ADD has when climbing? What if they had emphasized safety, when climbing, to the point that all of the climbers, all of the time, wore helmets?

What if Sean and his co-climbers saw clearly the risk associated with drinking before or during climbing? What if they saw clearly how alcohol can lead to poor judgment and loss of one's best physical coordination?

What if the treatment programs and/or consultants had a system that demanded change in the parents of the loved ones affected by alcohol and drugs? What if the young one was only the "identified" patient and the system of relationships surrounding the "identified patient" was the "actual patient" being treated?

What if the therapist at Sean's last treatment program had pushed Louella to confront fully her role as Sean's enabler?

What if the program in Washington State had refused to allow Louella to take Sean away before he was ready?

What if Sean's cousins had refused to drink with him? What if they had seen clearly the type of alcoholism from which he suffered, and supported him in his work toward sobriety?

What if relatives had confronted Louella with her enabling and encouraged her to stop? What if relatives would have refused to drink with Louella in support of Sean's efforts at sobriety?

What if Louella's family had accepted dyslexia as Sean's reality and fully supported Sean and his sacrificial and heroic efforts to learn to read? What if "Honor" is sometimes another word for "Pride" ???

What if Sean's mother had seen clearly the power of her role and her attitude in all three of Sean's issues?   What if she had fully supported -- with all the positive energy she could have mustered -- Sean and his Father in dealing with the dyslexia? What if Louella had mastered the list of "skills" needed to live with ADD and systematically taught them to her son – with a joy-filled and thankful attitude at being given the knowledge to help? What if Louella refused to support Sean in his destructive drinking and drug use, while pouring into him affirmation for his other, many talents and abilities?

****

286

To paraphrase the psychologist Gary Chapman[18], human behavior is motivated by certain emotional and spiritual needs. When we don't understand the needs of others, we fail to understand his or her behavior.

When someone complains that you don't give him enough time, he is asking for love (in the form of your time). When another says "I don't ever do anything right," she is begging for love (in the form of affirming words).

When we argue about the *behavior*, we often stimulate more negative behavior. Look *behind* the behavior to discover the emotional need. Then, meet that need, and you will eliminate the negative behavior.

My friend struggled. He came to realize that he had failed - - over and over – to see and respond to the needs of others, the needs that lie behind their behaviors.

He failed in his relationship with Louella and he failed in his relationship with Sean.

His own list of "What ifs" dwarfs the list above.

He is haunted by his own list.

He was able to go on in life only by having hope in a merciful God.

****

---

[18] From his book "The One Year Love Language Minute Devotional."

Mariah, you can make your own list of "what if's" from the story of your Dad. Imagine how Sean's life might have been different given any, several, or all of the "what if's." Use your own "what if's" and/or the above "what if's."

This is not an exercise of wasted time wishing the past were different. Rather, it is an opportunity to learn. An exercise in considering options. A recognition that our choices have consequences. A chance to learn from the past so that the future may be better, and more positive, and with less regrets.

LESSONS 7 -- YOUR GRANDDAD WAS HAUNTED
OR, DON'T HOLD TOO RIGIDLY TO DREAMS

This little story has two parts.

In the first part, you will see your Granddad's attitude toward learning. Some of his wisdom is there.

In the second part is a lesson to be learned. Certainly, as he looked back he felt he could have taken a different approach that might have made a difference for his son.

It was one night some weeks after your Dad died. Your Granddad and I had gone up to a rural place in the mountains, to get away.

We weren't gone long. Just overnight. A long period away from productive activity wasn't your Grandfather's way of living life. He always had something to do.

But he had made a promise some weeks earlier to someone he loved. He was a person who kept his promises. As best he could, he kept his promises.

We were up at a Bed and Breakfast. A place called *Sueños Encantados*, 4.5 miles south of Cuba, New Mexico.

While up there some things he experienced triggered thoughts in him. Those thoughts in turn generated feelings. He became very sad. It became clear to me how deeply things were eating at him. He was mourning a whole lot of things, even as he was mourning the loss of your Dad.

To understand what triggered the feelings inside of him, let me try, as best I can, to recreate how we ended up there and what we experienced. I think this story will tell you a bit more about your Grandfather. And, I think it will tell you a little bit about the life that he had hoped to have with your Father.

How did we end up there?

One day, a few weeks after your Dad died, a patient came to see him. This was a patient that your Granddad was pretty fond of. Your Grandfather had met him about ten years earlier, as a patient. That was when he was working for a community health clinic then called FirstChoice, in Albuquerque.

Actually, this man's children and his wife had seen your Granddad first as patients. The children were then in grade school. The wife was a teacher. My friend told me he thought the wife was very pretty, very smart, and very nice.

She and your Granddad had some things in common. They both had children about the same age. They both had a son and a daughter. They were both Catholics. They both appreciated education and learning. Seems they both appreciated hard work, too.

One time, some years back, she came in to see him and she was studying as she waited to be seen. When he came into the exam room, he asked what she was reading. It turned out that she was studying "How to Learn." He asked about it. She shared.

He asked her for a copy of the notes or outline. She agreed.

When it came to learning he had immediately thought of his children. He hoped to share this "How to Learn" system with both of his children.

Your Granddad had come to believe (from his own father[19]) that the very most important thing to learn was – _how to learn_. He would repeatedly share that belief with his two children.

Sadly , Sean had come to HATE formal learning. Part of his negative attitude came from his problem with dyslexia. The other part came from his mother's attitude toward formal book learning. She didn't take to it much.

Because of the dyslexia, reading was hard for him. So he didn't like to do it. Instead of support and encouragement from his mother, she would empathize with his suffering and allow him to minimize his efforts.

---

[19] That would have been your great-Grandfather, John Joseph Hennelly, the one who came over from Ireland.

She may have meant well, but she actually added to his suffering.

Sean came to believe that he wasn't smart, which wasn't true at all. He was plenty bright and plenty capable. But, the reality was that because of the dyslexia, he would have to put in more time and effort to accomplish what others could learn more easily and quickly.

Sean came to the mistaken belief that ease of learning indicated how smart a person was.

OK, now I know that I got off of my story about what led to us being up on the ranch near Cuba, NM, and what was haunting your Granddad. But I'll get there.

When we get older, sometimes we see the importance of taking a side trip while we are getting to where we're going. It enriches life. And life is way too short not to be enriched and enjoyed.

The loss of his son reminded my friend of this with the force of a sledgehammer to the head. After your Dad died, my friend would sometimes kind of wander through things as he shared with me.

Well, this patient did, indeed, bring him a copy of her notes, at the time of her next office visit. And your Granddad shared them with both the kids. You could ask Sean's sister for a copy of them, I think Maria-Teresa still has them.

OK, so that's the part of this story about learning, Mariah. Your Granddad wants you to be sure to "learn how to learn."

The second part of the story has to do with the memories and reflections triggered in your Granddad.

Well it was actually her husband, the patient's husband, who came in to the office to see your Grandfather a few weeks before the trip to *Sueños Encantados*. This man had been through his own nightmare since your Grandfather first met him. He was found to have a problem that progressed over several years to the point that he required both a brain surgery and a kidney transplant!

Your Granddad admired him greatly.

They visited as friends during the office appointment. Grandpa wanted to know how he was doing, not just as a patient, but as a person.

Your Grandfather learned he had retired from his job due to the medical issues, and that he was spending more time at his parents' ranch, south of Cuba, where they had started a Bed and Breakfast. They called it *Sueños Encantados.*

My friend thought that might be a great place to "get away" and to keep his promise.

He got the name and number from his patient, called the parents, and made arrangements.

Several weeks later, up we went.

What my friend experienced up there was what prompted the thoughts and feelings – and reflections.

The patient's parents had retired to the home of his mom's family. The place had been homesteaded by her great Grandfather. It had all the history of a Spanish family of Northern New Mexico oozing out of the vigas, latias, and adobes.

To a willing observer all the work, sacrifice, and love of family, over several generations, was visible. The fields had to have been cleared, work done before there were tractors. The small stream that supplied the water which made life there possible had to be directed by hand dug ditches. The thick-walled adobe buildings were needed to make it through the cold winters before modern heating conveniences. The buildings had to have been done by hand: crafted for function and practicality as well as esthetics.

The founding father – the "patron" had homesteaded the place and started his family there after the Civil War. He was granted the land for his role in the Union military. And, he is buried there too. A resting place close to the buildings he had constructed.

As your Granddad experienced the place, he remembered how he had sacrificed for and dreamed of his own "place" in Espanola. A place on which he had hoped to raise a family with a loving, hard-working, and supportive wife.

Your Grandfather had eight and one half acres of land with a deed documenting ownership all the way back to the king of Spain[20]. He had repaired the irrigation ditches. He had brought the water back and rejuvenated the land. He had put up fences to rotate pastures for horses – one for each member of the family (even one for the baby they were expecting: Sean). He had all the saddles and the horse trailer and the four-wheeled drive vehicle to take them up into the beautiful mountains that surround "the place." He was about to finish a 1000 square foot addition to the old adobe (and planned more additions, for his young family).

Oh, my friend still owned the property. But it was no longer his "place." He had sacrificed for it. But the dreams had never been realized.

He had moved the family away and not returned, because there was not the love, hard-work, and support he assumed would be there.

For dreams to be realized….

Well, his dreams didn't happen. And, he realized up there at *Sueños Encantados* he had never completely given up those dreams.

Now he had to do so.

His son, Sean, was dead.

That reality was forcing him to see what he should have seen years earlier.

---

[20] Curiously, the King of Spain had "given" the land that was "taken" (if you will) from the native peoples who preceded the Europeans.

He should have sold "the place" in Espanola years ago. He should not have worked so hard to hold onto "the place" and his dream. He should have eased his financial pressures and allowed himself to have more time and energy for his family.

Holding on to his dream had been a mistake.

All too clear. All too late.

Your Grandfather loved Sean and he loved his family. The life he had dreamed of having with your Dad wasn't ever going to happen. Not later. Not ever. His heart ached.

What he would have done if he did not know there was a God…

He was haunted by the loss of his dreams.

Funny, he thought: *Sueños Encantados* (Enchanted Dreams). How appropriate.

LESSONS 8 -- PERSONAL CHALLENGES

As you learned in the story, your Dad had three very
specific, identifiable problems. Let's look briefly at a
healthy attitude toward each one. This is important because
some or all of them may affect you (or your children).

About Dyslexia
Mariah, if you grow up to have dyslexia[21] you should not
feel embarrassed or dishonored by it. You too are a
beautiful creation of God, just as your Dad is. That
beautiful creation may have a challenge or a problem or an
issue (whatever label you wish to use) known as Dyslexia.
But you must realize you are not the challenge, you are not
the problem, you are not the issue. The dyslexia is. Deal
with it. Develop a "can-do" attitude. With a "can-do"
attitude you can and will learn to live with it.

Sean worked very hard to learn to read. He had a
wonderful tutor. He did a remarkable job in learning to
read so well. Tragically, he sacrificed many, many hours at
an age where he could and should have been learning other
things as well. He missed many experiences that would
have helped him mature; mature with more joy and less
turmoil.

---

[21] Remember, the form of dyslexia that your Dad had is an inherited
form of dyslexia. So it may have been passed on to you with the other
genes that gave you life. Also, remember that this form seems to be
milder in girls than in boys. And, because it is inherited, it is possible
that you could pass it on to a child of yours.

297

Mariah, don't let anyone else's (mistaken) belief or attitude let you feel negative or bad or inferior or embarrassed or dishonored by dyslexia, if you have it[22].

About Attention Deficit Disorder

Mariah, if you find that you have Attention Deficit Disorder, do the same thing as suggested above. Accept it. Admit it. It does not have you, you have it.

Adopt the "can-do" attitude. Learn about ADD and learn about how to live with it. Remember that you are a child of God. You are precious and beautiful. ADD can be lived with. It can be dealt with. You are NOT defined by ADD or any other challenge or limitation.

Your Grandfather saw patient after patient who did very, very well in life with a diagnosis of ADD. Almost universally, if property diagnosed, a student will improve with treatment. In school this is exhibited by better grades. It was common to see an improvement from grades of F and D to C and B. Or from C average to A or A- average.

Your Granddad is certain Sean could have done this (a) if he had consistently used mediations ("pills") and (b) if he had a properly structured environment within which to live and function ("skills"). Two parents, united, both valuing education, and working to create a supportive environment with appropriate boundaries, can allow a child to grow up strong, confident, and capable, despite ADD.

---

[22] Another, inspiring, Gospel story comes to mind here: Gospel of John, Chapter 9, verses 1-3.

A person is not defined or determined by what limitations, challenges, or characteristics – favorable or unfavorable – are bestowed on him or her from beyond their control. Rather, it is how the individual deals with life and its challenges that determine his or her character.

About Addiction

Mariah, it seems that both your genetic mother and father suffered with alcohol and drug problems. It is quite possible, indeed likely, that you have inherited a genetic makeup which puts you at risk for developing the same problems. You can decide, with the "can-do", positive attitude to minimize your risks. One simple way is to not drink any alcohol or use any drugs.[23] Just never do it.

My friend liked to share two things with his patients who had alcoholism, or who were at risk of developing alcoholism.

1) He would challenge them to consider "What can you do when you are drinking that you cannot do when you are not drinking?"

---

[23] This might be the wisest thing because of some studies. Those studies show that, in a person predisposed to alcoholism, when the person drinks, a chemical builds up in the brain AND CANNOT GET OUT of the brain. That chemical trapped in the brain may be the reason the alcoholic craves drinking. Thus, if a predisposed person NEVER drinks then that chemical never gets trapped in the brain, and the person has no cravings which they have to do battle with. If it turns out that this is the true (chemical) cause to alcoholism, then the more alcohol one drinks the more of that chemical builds up in the brain and the harder the battle is to fight.

He was trying to get them to THINK about what
benefit they were receiving from drinking alcohol.

Mariah, think about that question for yourself.

2)   He would tell them the following story from his
own life experience.

The first week he was in medical school was a
series of orientation activities. In the first couple of
days, he and his fellow students (about 100 in all)
were told that they would be graded in medical
school on a "pass-fail" basis. They were reminded
that each was an extremely bright person with
virtually no chance of flunking out of medical
school. The school and the teachers were going to
provide whatever support was needed to assure each
new student that they would graduate.

As a result, he and his fellow students were to
consider themselves, already, as "physicians."
Well, that was nice, and reassuring, and flattering to
a new medical student.

However, a few short days later they were given
additional information that was not so desirable.
They were told -- that as physicians -- they were
now proud members of a profession that had one of
the highest risks of divorce, suicide, alcoholism, and
drug addiction.

Whew, your Granddad hadn't signed up for those
problems. This information caused him to reflect.
And he reasoned as follows:

He wasn't married; so (at least at that point in his life) he was not at risk for divorce.
He didn't, nor had he ever, felt depressed; so (at least at that time) he need not worry about suicide.
He had not used, nor had he ever intended to use, drugs; so that didn't seem to be an issue.
However, alcoholism was a different matter.

In college, he had, at times, on Friday or Saturday evenings, or over holiday breaks from school responsibilities, drank too much. The drinking never seemed to interfere with his duties. But he knew he drank too much from time to time; and that he didn't need to do so.

When he heard what his medical school professor related, he made up his mind to determine if he had a problem with alcohol. He devised a test for himself. He would not drink any alcohol for one year; and see if he could do this. He would see if abstaining from alcohol negatively affected his life. Though he would stop alcohol, he decided he would not change anything else in his life. He would continue with the same friends (some of whom might drink – even over drink - from time to time), continue to play soccer with the two teams (where he would almost certainly be offered beer from teammates), he would continue to go to the same social gatherings (some of which would include alcohol), including going to "watering holes[24]."

He told himself that if he could not go a year without alcohol than he would make further adjustments to prove to himself that alcohol was not needed to enjoy life (or that, for him, alcohol had control over him).

He went the whole year. And, to his amazement, no one realized he had stopped alcohol. None of his friends, none of his family.

He came to realize and experience that alcohol was not needed to enjoy life.

When the year was over he allowed himself to resume drinking. However, he never again drank with anything even close to the frequency and quantity he had in college. Never again did he have more than a couple of drinks at a time.

Mariah, if you chose to drink alcohol (and I hope you fine no good reason to do so) and you cannot control it, then stop drinking – because, if you can't stop, then it controls you.

As was shared above, regarding dyslexia and ADD, so too with alcohol or drugs (or any other "label" or problem, for that matter), Mariah, you are not defined by a problem. You and your life are defined by God and by HOW YOU DEAL WITH PROBLEMS.

---

[24] Bars and night spots that serve alcohol.

LESSONS 9 -- POSSIBLE EXPLANATIONS

Why bother to explain, or even to try to explain?

Your Grandpa was gifted in science and mathematics. Just as Sean's learning style was Visual-Spatial, so Grandpa's was Logical-Mathematical.

He could never understand why others, including and particularly Louella, would make decisions and take actions that made no sense and were contrary to professed goals or desires.

As you have seen from the story, many such irrational choices were critical to Sean's life.

For Grandpa these harmful and destructive acts begged explanation.

Over the years Grandpa had repeatedly tried to make sense of such behavior. And, he repeatedly attempted to influence and to alter the thinking associated with such foolishness. Unfortunately, as the years went by, he met with more and more resistance. One could say he met with more and more failure.

Yet, he never stopped questioning. He couldn't stop. It was his nature to ask why.

Eventually, he came across two logical explanations for illogical behavior.

One came from reading; and it came about a year before Sean's death. The other came from listening; and that came only weeks after Sean's death. Sadly, neither arrived in time to improve Sean's predicament.

Mariah, by the time you are old enough to read this, these two "Explanations" may be commonly understood and accepted. Or, they may have been rejected as unfounded. Or, possibly, other -- new and more insightful -- explanations may have emerged.

Despite the possibility these explanations may be discounted with time, your Grandfather felt compelled to have me add these to the book. Again, his goal lies in the possibly of helping you and/or others.

The two explanations may seem different. However, upon closer scrutiny they may simply be the same, just expressed differently.

The first possible explanation for illogical behavior your Granddad found in Malcolm Baldridge's book "Outliers." In one section of the book the author lays out an example of how HONOR can be the basis for destructive, irrational choices.

Years ago, before advances in transportation, there were numerous isolated hamlets tucked away in the Appalachian Mountains. A destructive pattern of interacting developed in one small isolated community after another along that stretch of rugged mountains. The classic example is the well-known story of the "Hatfields and McCoys." However, a study of history showed this prototype of conflict and violence was not unique to one set of feuding clans. Rather it was repeated over and over in the area.

Baldridge describes, in some detail, how illogical decision after illogical decision unreasonably prolonged interfamily quarrels and disputes in those mountains. Offers and opportunities to end hostilities were repeatedly rejected in favor of continued revenge. As a result, pain, suffering, and loss of life went on for generations.

Why were openings for compromise and for ending the cycles of violence repeatedly rejected? When studied by psychologists, the explanation for such potentially suicidal choices was "honor."

Other terms for "honor" might be respect or pride -- even fairness, integrity, or public esteem. Once he read this, your Grandfather recognized this as the explanation for illogical gang behavior in the present. Suspects claim they were "dis'ed" as the rationale for revenge attacks and killings. "Being 'dis'ed'" meaning one has been disrespected or dishonored.

Once he saw this clearly, my friend began to think this sense of -- or need for -- "honor" could explain what he saw as the inexplicable response to Sean's diagnosis of dyslexia. Could it be that crucial members of Louella's family, including Louella herself[25], saw Sean's dyslexia and its genetic origin in her family as a negative label that dishonored or disrespected them?

---

[25] As exhibited by her failure to ever change from her lack of support for your Granddad and his views in the presence of her family.

This is not merely a curiosity. For this split (and its basis), between Louella and himself, over how to live with and respond to the diagnosis of dyslexia in Sean, was the nexus of the conflict which destroyed the family peace and unity: peace and unity that Sean should have enjoyed.

Unfortunately, as I said, Grandfather came to this clear understanding many years after the destruction had taken its toll on Sean, and only months before his death.

My friend sensed that had he appreciated "honor" as an explanation for others' response to Sean's diagnosis, the outcome might have been different. Among the possibilities, your Granddad believed he would not have been so incredulous. And, even though he still would have vigorously disagreed with the Roybals' self-deprecating view, he would have been more understanding and empathetic. With and from a different frame of reference, he might have won them over to his views and thereby gained their support for Sean.

A second explanation can be found in "Cognitive Dissonance Theory."

What is Cognitive Dissonance?

Kendra Cherry, in the online reference "About.com", answers the question very succinctly in this way:

What Is Cognitive Dissonance?

Answer:

People tend to seek consistency in their beliefs and perceptions. So what happens when one of our beliefs conflicts with another previously held belief? The term cognitive dissonance is used to describe the feeling of discomfort that results from holding two conflicting beliefs. When there is a discrepancy between beliefs and behaviors, something must change in order to eliminate or reduce the dissonance.

Examples of Cognitive Dissonance
Cognitive dissonance can occur in many areas of life, but it is particularly evident in situations where an individual's behavior conflicts with beliefs that are integral to his or her self-identity. For example, consider a situation in which a woman who values financial security is in a relationship with a man who is financially irresponsible.

The conflict:
- It is important for her to be financially secure.
- She is dating a man who is financially unstable.

In order to reduce this dissonance between belief and behavior, she can either leave the relationship or reduce her emphasis on financial security. In the case of the second option, dissonance could be further minimized by emphasizing the positive qualities of her significant other rather than focusing on his perceived flaws.

A more common example of cognitive dissonance occurs in the purchasing decisions we make on a regular basis. Most people want to hold the belief they make good choices. When a product or item we purchase turns out badly, it conflicts with our previously existing belief about our decision-making abilities.

Why is Cognitive Dissonance Important?

Cognitive dissonance plays a role in many value judgments, decisions and evaluations. Becoming aware of how conflicting beliefs impact the decision-making process is a great way to improve your ability to make faster and more accurate choices.

What is important to grasp, Mariah, is that "Cognitive dissonance theory warns that people have a bias to seek consonance among their cognitions. This bias gives the theory its predictive power, ***shedding light on otherwise puzzling irrational and even destructive behavior***."[26] (Emphasis added).

According to recent studies in the area of Cognitive Dissonance, when given a choice between emotional ties and facts, the facts will lose almost every time. When facts and feelings disagree, facts get thrown out. One doesn't reject the facts because they are facts, but because accepting the facts is painful.

Other recent studies indicate that when people are more self-confident they are capable of taking in conflicting

---

[26] This is from *Wikipedia*, which gives a more detailed description.

views -- or views that challenged earlier beliefs -- and living with the conflict.[27]

Over the years, my friend couldn't understand how or why Louella would continue to make decisions harmful to those she claimed to love. Or why Sean would repeatedly make choices that were illogical and harmful. As stated above, Cognitive Dissonance Theory sheds "light on otherwise puzzling irrational and even destructive behavior."

Mariah, it would be very instructional for you to go back to the story and fine those situations where illogical choices were made.   See if you can now make some sense out of them, based on the above explanations.

Your Grandfather found himself doing just that. Painfully, it was as a result of his holding the mirror before himself.

Why had he not gone to court with Sean, after Sean's success for over a year in Prescott? Why had he not rejected Sean's staying with Louella, thereby tempting them both? Why had he assumed Sean had not resumed drinking after the end of house arrest?

Your Grandfather explains these things in the story. He made assumptions. My friend's explanation itself begs to be understood. Why would he make such assumptions in the face of the history of repeated facts that make those assumptions unlikely?

Your Granddad assumed Sean knew he was proud of his son and his son's accomplishments. Granddad assumed

---

[27] From a National Public Radio audio article on "Cognitive Dissonance."

Sean would see the risk in living with Louella for "house arrest" -- and Louella and the judge would too – and Sean would have asked the judge to stay with his Father. Granddad assumed Sean had learned enough from his year and a half of sobriety and treatment to reject further drinking and drugs.

The facts do not support your Granddad's assumptions. So, why did he make them?

The Theory of Cognitive Dissonance can explain such assumptions.

My friend never imagined, with his background and education, with his self-image and world view, with his pride and his desire for public esteem, that he (Granddad) would have such a dysfunctional family. His feelings – his desire for things to be different from what they were – conflicted with the facts – the way things were. The facts lost out.

These explanations helped your Grandfather to make sense out of senseless choices. Unfortunately, they came to be clearly understood only in the months just before and just after Sean's death. Had he been aware earlier, might he have conducted himself differently, and might the outcome for Sean have been different?

You, Mariah, have the opportunity to learn from the mistakes of others.

LESSONS 10 -- NOT ANY ONE INDIVIDUAL'S FAULT

Mariah, your Dad's death was not caused by any one individual. No one consciously or intentionally caused him to make the decisions he did that day. And Sean certainly planned on coming down from the rocks as physically healthy as when he went up. However, from the story -- and the lessons -- it should be clear to you that lots of individuals made choices which had unintended and negative consequences. Choices leading to unintended but negative consequences are known as "mistakes." It is heartbreaking to realize the most crucial mistakes were made by Sean and by those who loved him the most.

Your Grandfather did not know how long he himself would live. He wanted to be sure these things were written so that you could read them at the right time, when you were older.

He felt the lessons in each of the mistakes could help guide and protect you. He hoped you would not just read what he left you but that you would also study it, think about it, and possibly even share it. Be willing to share it with anyone, Mariah, who could be aided or helped by reading it. Your Grandfather prayed that some good would come from the tragic, unnecessary death of his son; by seeing the mistakes that were committed – some could be considered evils or sins; and by learning from them.

One of the most import lessons he wanted you to learn was the importance of developing and keeping the "can-do" attitude in life.

Such an attitude is positive and empowering. With this attitude one goes through life scanning for possibilities. One is open to new ideas. Such a "can-do" person is willing to change.

When faced with problems, conflicts, or barriers, the person with that attitude looks for ways to deal with or work around obstacles. She finds ways to keep moving forward. A "can-do" person develops self-discipline. She follows through on her commitments and her promises, especially those made to herself.

The "can-do" person looks at the world as a gift of opportunities from God.

The "can-do" attitude is life giving.

The "can-do" person has the potential to lead.

In writings about the best leader the world has ever know, the gospel (or good news) of Jesus, the Messiah, we are told the parable of the talents (Gospel of Matthew 25:14-30) and the parable of the gold coins (Gospel of Luke 19:12-27). In each of those parables Jesus contrasts the two attitudes. Take some time to read and ponder those parables.

Your Grandfather wants only the best for you, as he did for his son.

In this book you have read of many mistakes. Some smaller, some larger. Some by people not so close to your Dad. Some by people close to your Dad – including those to whom God had entrusted your Dad.

Again, Mariah, please learn from their mistakes.

> *"A wise woman learns from the mistakes of others.*
> *The average woman learns from her own mistakes.*
> *The foolish woman never learns."*

ADDENDUM

At the time of his death Sean was beginning to assume the responsibilities of being a father. He was, once again, following behavior he was taught, as well as, like all of us, selfish confusion. The most important aspects of fatherhood are spiritual and moral: building a relationship with God and building one's character. Unfortunately those two areas were underemphasized and supplanted by material aspects of parenthood. Yet one sensed the nobility of his actions and the movement within him to the "most important."

In this assumption of parenthood is repeated the same pattern delineated in the book. Sean does not make a wise choice (in assuming his fatherhood), and he is let down by those around him (who do not give him mature adult advice in so doing).

You see, it turned out that the little girl was not Sean's biological child.

The truth is that Sean was in an intimate relationship with her mother about the time of her conception. Thus, he had reason to suspect that she was his child. His decision to assume parental responsibilities for the little girl shows the kind-hearted nature that Sean had, and his growing willingness to accept responsibility for his actions. However, the decision was impulsive and imprudent.

The little girl's maternal grandmother was caregiver and surrogate mother. She saw Sean's compassion and willingness to collaborate with her. She became absolutely convinced that Sean was the child's father. She was going to move to Prescott with the little girl so that they would be close to "her father."

Sean's mother, too, bought into the charade. She did not guide Sean with wise counsel in first seeking the truth. Rather, she fully participated with the other two in leading the child into believing that Sean was her father.

All this was done despite the protestations of the child's biological mother, who was certain that Sean was not the father and had told each of them so. Unfortunately, her credibility was lacking for she suffered from problems that lead to repeated lying so as to manipulate others.

And where was my friend, Sean's father? He had not followed through after getting Sean settled into Prescott (as I described in the book). He, too, was not there to give his son sensible advice, albeit for very different reasons.

The truth became known after my friend had conceived and communicated this book. My friend was led to believe he had a grandchild, a living connection to his lost son. He felt the obligation to hold all that is shared in the book for the sake of this little girl, who would grow up without knowing her father.

Yet, even as my friend did his best to think of the child's future, he also felt a strong need to know the truth. He was able to take action that led to genetic testing that proved Sean was not the biological parent.

More pain.

More pain for all involved came when this truth was learned.

But much less pain than would have happened should this truth have become known years later.

My friend asked that I modify the book. Which I did. For example, the little girl's name is not Mariah, nor her mother's name Rina.

However, he did not want to abandon the book for he was convinced that others might and could learn from his mistakes, and the mistakes of others.

AFTERWORD

This book was written by me pseudonymously, as Ford O'Kenaly.

I did so for several reasons that are conscious to me.

I was too close to the events, both personally and in time. The pain of writing in the first person was too great to allow me to do so.

In addition, I could see the events and relationships from multiple and different points-of-view. My pseudonymous writer could express those varying perspectives in ways that "I" – in the first person -- could not. I could not do so without entering into convoluted explanations. And such explanations, I believe, would have detracted from the flow and from the essence of what I desired to communicate.

Words are but a limited way to share the totality of experience. And, for me, a further hindrance has been my limited verbal expertise and lack of preparation for such communication.

I have done my best. I am certain of the limitations inherent in this attempt at communication.

Still, I pray that others, even if but one soul, can learn from what I have written and thereby avoid pain and suffering similar to that which was not avoided in the lives of Sean and those who were close to him.

Michael Mark Hennelly, father of Sean-Michael Hennelly.

A REQUEST

Sean never met his grandfather, John Joseph Hennelly, who was gone before Sean was conceived. When he was a teenager, John J. Hennelly came over from rural, western Ireland with his younger sister Mary to seek a better life in America.

They settled in St. Louis, Missouri, where Mary became a nurse and eventually married. She and her husband Bernard Concannon had seven children. Bernard died prematurely and Mary raised those seven alone.

When my friend's Concannon cousins learned of Sean's death, they pooled their gifts and made a generous donation to "Boys Hope Girls Hope."

The organization's MISSION: "Boys Hope Girls Hope helps academically capable and motivated children-in-need to meet their full potential and become men and women for others by providing value-centered, family-like homes, opportunities and education through college."

- The organization's STATEMENT OF VALUES: "Founded on the belief that a loving God cares about the life of every individual, Boys Hope Girls Hope acts in accordance with the following values:Education is critical to reaching one's full potential.
- Spirituality and an active faith-life are essential elements of healthy personal development.

- Children have the capacity to transcend their circumstances if given a safe environment, opportunities, and loving support.
- Integrity, honesty, respect, a willingness to love, and service to others are important measures of personal success.
- Individuals are responsible for their destinies and actions, and all children deserve the guidance, support and opportunities to choose a path to reaching their full potential.
- Respect for the dignity, value, unique perspectives, and talents of every individual is the foundation of positive social and emotional development, as well as strong and vibrant communities."

Boys Hope Girls Hope is an organization helping youngsters facing issues that are in many ways similar to those of Sean-Michael. I ask you to thoughtfully consider a donation to the work of Boys Hope Girls Hope.

Their website is
http://www.boyshopegirlshope.org/Home.aspx

www.ingramcontent.com/pod-product-compliance
Lightning Source LLC
Chambersburg PA
CBHW030531100426
42813CB00001B/217